HOW TO AVOID
H.E.N.R.Y.
(HIGH EARNER NOT RICH YET)
SYNDROME®

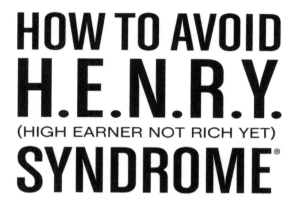

HOW TO AVOID
H.E.N.R.Y.
(HIGH EARNER NOT RICH YET)
SYNDROME®

Financial Strategies to Own Your Future

GIDEON DRUCKER, CFP®
Director, Drucker Wealth Builder

Redwood Publishing, LLC
Orange County, California

Published by Redwood Publishing, LLC
Orange County, California
www.redwooddigitalpublishing.com
info@redwooddigitapublishing.com

Printed in the United States of America

First Printing, 2020

ISBN 978-1-952106-05-7 (hardcover)
ISBN 978-1-952106-06-4 (paperback)
ISBN 978-1-952106-07-1 (e-book)

Library of Congress Cataloguing Number: 2020900916

Book Design:
    Cover Design: Michelle Manley
    Interior Design: Ghislain Viau
    Chapter image by Ryan DeBerardinis on ShutterStock.com

First Edition

10 9 8 7 6 5 4 3 2 1

To my jump school commander...

You said you could push me or I could jump out of the plane...you said jumping will make me a stronger man...Thank you for allowing me to jump!

To my army brothers, commanders, and officers...

In the hopes that you'll read this and realize that I'm a better Financial planner than I was a Soldier

To the future Mrs. Drucker who I haven't met yet...

My mom thinks we're going to meet "any day now"... so be ready

To my late Poppy Sy and Poppy Bernie...

You built a strong, loving family that's there for each other always...We are where we are because of you.

To my mom, dad, and Gabby...

You three are not just my family but my three best friends in the world...I can think of nothing on Earth I'm more thankful for.

Contents

My Invitation:
This Is Why We Plan

You're excited. Motivated. And committed to building the future that you imagine. But you're also not quite sure how you're going to get there. Maybe you have student loans bulldozing half of your paycheck. Perhaps that first home you were aiming to buy at age thirty-five seems like it's only getting further away when it should be in your line of sight. Maybe you're pregnant and wondering how you and your partner are going to be able to afford college for your children in eighteen years. Perhaps that six-figure salary you were so excited to earn after so much hard work barely seems like enough to make a crack in your savings.

In other words, maybe, you are a H.E.N.R.Y.: a High Earner who's Not Rich Yet.

If that six-figure salary you are finally earning after so much work barely seems like enough to make a crack in your savings, you could be a H.E.N.R.Y.; A High Earner who's Not Rich Yet.

This book, and really my entire motivation to create the H.E.N.R.Y. Syndrome® and build my business around the idea, can be traced back to the third day of my career and an innocuous comment by a new client named Steve.

During my first week at my family's wealth management firm, I was sitting in on a meeting with my dad, Lance, our firm's president and CEO; Kitty Richie, our director of wealth management; and two new clients, Steve and Jodi, who were in our office for the third time. As you can imagine, three days into "the business," I wasn't there so much for my wit and wisdom, but to learn our process (and to take notes, as my dad would want you to know). Steve and Jodi were a nice couple in their early sixties and only a few years away from retirement. They had done well for themselves, each earning a healthy six-figure income throughout their prime earning years. They'd sent all three of their children to college and lived an affluent but not ostentatious lifestyle, spending money without too much thought or stress over the years. That said, they were in our office for a plan delivery meeting (a financial checkup), because they didn't have any idea when they could comfortably retire, and what that

retirement would look like when they ultimately chose to step off the wheel.

My dad reviewed their cash flow, budget, and variable expenses, as well as their existing investments. He then analyzed their sources of income in retirement, and walked them through their written financial plan; a plan broken out into a number of different timelines that were dependent on their choices and the resultant realities that could play out in the coming twenty-five to thirty years.

As the meeting concluded, Steve and Jodi breathed a deep sigh of relief; they were going to be fine. Yes, they had to cut back their spending over the next five or so years, and, yes, realistically, they each had to work an extra two years to afford the retirement lifestyle they truly wanted, but all in all, they were on the right track. It was an intense, emotional, but ultimately cathartic two hours for our new clients to understand what the next phase of their lives would entail.

As Steve walked out, he mentioned that he was relieved to have a better sense of their financial situation, and while he was aware that there was work ahead of them, he and Jodi felt ready to get it done. Then, off the cuff, he chuckled the words that would come to epitomize my greatest motivation for the future: "If only I had met you and thought more about my financial goals thirty years ago—woo! Imagine where we would be!"

I spent the next six months sitting in on practically all of my dad's meetings as a way of learning our business, and

I heard this exact lament dozens of times. Sometimes, it was casual and uttered with a reflective chuckle by someone who was ultimately going to be fine, like Steve, but a lot of times it was said with devastating realism, as these new clients were left pondering past choices and contemplating how vastly different their family's financial picture could have been.

"If only I had met you back then."

This became my rallying cry. I thought about my sister, my friends, my fraternity brothers, the guys I'd served with in my Israeli Paratroopers unit, and my extended universe of young professionals, and felt, *Not them. I will do everything I can to make sure that none of them ever has that doubt, pain, or guilt about starting too late. They will be prepared.*

And then I thought beyond my little universe. What if we could change that cycle of financial procrastination for the masses? What if Steve and Jodi didn't just find out if they were on the right track at sixty-three, but rather at thirty (and every year thereafter as their lives evolved)? What if we could have reached Steve and Jodi when they were at the bottom of their mountain, looking up at their vast journey ahead?

This is why I'm here.

Before we get started, try to imagine, if only for a moment, where you're going to be thirty years from now. What are you hoping to have achieved as you're sitting there at sixty years old, a few years away from retirement (and reading the fifteenth edition of this book)? What will have been your greatest financial accomplishments? Was it buying that first dream house with a white picket fence and beautiful backyard that your kids got to run around in throughout their entire childhood? Did it mean paying for your son or daughter to attend the college of his or her dreams without having to deal with the burden of student loans, like you had to do? Were you able to help your own parents, who sacrificed so much for you to succeed, be able to retire with dignity? Or maybe it was just being able to comfortably afford that extravagant two-week vacation to Italy each summer with your partner?

This is what it's all about. This is why we plan. This is the fun stuff that motivates all of us. Your vision of the future is why you're working hard, making money, and building your career. Whether these goals are years away or decades away, I know one indisputable fact: the sooner you start thinking, planning, and making active decisions

> Your vision of the future is why you're working hard, making money, and building your career. Whether these goals are years away or decades away, I know one indisputable fact: the sooner you start thinking, planning, and making active decisions in your financial life, the closer you will be to turning your vision into a reality.

in your financial life, the closer you will be to turning your vision into a reality. If this book and the lessons contained within it help you to take that first step toward the future of your dreams, I will consider this venture both a worthwhile endeavor and an extraordinary success.

— Gideon Drucker, CFP®

1

My Journey and Yours

"Money, if it does not bring you happiness, will at least help you be miserable in comfort."
– Helen Gurley Brown

I grew up in a unique family. My dad and my grandfather were focused (although "obsessed" may be a more accurate word) not so much on money…but on the power of proper planning for one's financial future. It was never about the things that money can buy (cars, homes, luxury vacations), but, rather, the peace of mind that comes from having a plan, sticking to the plan, and knowing that you and your loved ones will one day reap the benefits of that plan. As the founder of Drucker Wealth Management, my grandpa Bernie was obsessed with financial planning, which manifested itself not just in relation to my family, but through his work on behalf of the thousands of individuals and families over the years that he was fortunate enough to work with.

Growing up as a Drucker, I've lived with this planning mindset my whole life, and so, in many ways, this book feels like it's three generations in the making. It's the fulfillment of sixty years of commitment, sacrifice, and, ultimately, financial independence achieved by my hero (my dad) and his hero (his dad). I'm humbled beyond words that I get to share the timeless principles that have guided them both through the decades and that have inspired and motivated me to become a guide for our "next generation of clients"— those just starting out in their careers, with young families and new financial responsibilities.

So, who am I, and why should you be interested in what I have to say? Simply put, my whole world is about making sure that our generation of so-called millennials—today's young professionals—has a better understanding of our financial situation and what it will take to reach our financial goals. It's my mission to make sure that we all have realistic plans to start saving money and building wealth toward the ultimate achievement of both our immediate and more distant goals. Truth be told, we certainly have our work cut out

> My mission is to make sure that our generation of so-called millennials— today's young professionals—has a better understanding of our financial situation and what it will take to reach our financial goals.

for us. If all of the statistics we read every day are true, we're in pretty rough shape and have a challenging road ahead!

- Adjusted for inflation, the annual salary of a millennial today is an estimated 20 percent lower than the average salary for a baby boomer at the same age, according to a Smart Asset study that analyzed data from the Bureau of Labor Statistics for millennials who were ages sixteen to thirty-four in 2015.

- While millennials have benefited from a 67 percent rise in wages since 1970, according to research by Student Loan Hero, this increase hasn't kept up with inflating living costs: Rent, home prices, and college tuition have all increased faster than incomes in the US.

- Millennials are less wealthy than previous generations were at their age at any point between 1989 and 2007, according to The Economist, which cited a recent paper by the Brookings Institution. Median household wealth was roughly 25 percent lower for those ages twenty to thirty-five in 2016 than it was for the same age group in 2007.

- Meanwhile, a report by the Federal Reserve published in November found that millennials have much less money than Gen Xers and baby boomers had at their age: "Millennials are less well off than members of earlier generations when they were young, with lower earnings, fewer assets, and less wealth," the study said.

- Millennials born in the 1980s are at the greatest risk of becoming a "lost generation" for wealth accumulation, according to a 2018 report by the Federal Reserve Bank of St. Louis. The report also found that as of 2016, people born in this decade had wealth levels 34 percent below where they would most likely have been if the financial crisis hadn't occurred, the report found.[1]

These are some truly frightening numbers and a grim reality for way too many young people in America. I'm here to change that as best I can.

I'm in a unique position as the third-generation Drucker at my family's wealth management firm. As I alluded to earlier, my grandpa started our firm way back in 1959, when he first began working with families and individuals

who were looking to become financially independent over the course of their lives.

Now, sixty years later, our firm has grown exponentially, our business is thriving, and my dad, Lance, as president and CEO, is running the show, as he has for the past thirty-five years. While our phone number hasn't changed since the mid-1980s, we've grown into one of the top wealth management firms in the country, with a dedicated twelve-person team behind us and wonderful clients beside us—clients we genuinely enjoy meeting with and who have done pretty well for themselves over the years.

*My grandpa when he started (what was then called)
Drucker Financial on his own.*

Sixty years later, our DWM Family has grown considerably.

11

While I've been a part of this story for only a few years now, in many ways, it feels like I've been a part of Drucker Wealth since before I even knew exactly what we did.

Growing Up a Drucker

My dad has always been my hero. His work ethic, passion for life, unwavering confidence, and singular commitment to our family made him basically Superman to me, even when I was too young to have put it in those words. So naturally, as a kid, I wanted to know *everything* about his business.

(Fortunately) My dad and I don't dress alike as much in the office as we did when I was growing up.

I grew up going to my dad's financial workshops all over New York City, listening to client stories at the family dinner table, attending every client event and business conference I could, and badgering my dad about what we did and how we did it until he would explain every story, parable, and (to me) exciting detail. Throughout high school, university, and my military service, I was always reading, highlighting, and making notes in all of the financial planning books that had inspired my grandpa and dad throughout their careers—messages and timeless ideas that continue to guide us today. (Yup, I was way too intense and nerdy, even back then!)

The Drucker clan circa 2006,
with our beloved & much missed dog Madeline!

While learning the ins and outs of what my dad did day-to-day was interesting, far more impactful was the openness about money, opportunity, and our family's finances that my sister, Gabby, and I experienced growing up under my parents' roof. They talked about *everything* with us. As a result, by the time we went off to college, we had a real appreciation for the value of a dollar, had established disciplined saving habits, had started our own business teaching tennis together (seeing firsthand the value of being self-employed and letting our money work for us), and had developed our own intense desire to become financially independent.

Jumping Out of Planes in Israel

I took my talents to Lehigh University before deciding, in my senior year, to join the Israel Defense Forces upon graduation. Hold on! If you perked up or feel like I just started an entirely new story that doesn't totally track with what I've been building toward, you can only imagine how my mom felt the first time I told her I was considering joining the IDF! My motivation was simple: despite my not being religious, I've always grown up in a proud Jewish home, and I've always had a deep love and admiration for and connection with my brothers and sisters in Israel. Throughout my university years, I had done a lot of writing and public speaking on Israel's behalf, and I felt, at a certain point, that alone wasn't enough. To truly do my part, I had to walk the walk and defend Israel with my own sweat and blood. Most Israelis have to serve in the IDF, and I was committed to doing my part as well for the protection of my people.

Fast-forward two years and my time as a paratrooper in the IDF was the most challenging, both physically and mentally, of my life. Without question, however, it was

also the most rewarding and life affirming. My brothers and I spent weeks training in the desert, marching dozens of kilometers each night, eating little, and sleeping less. I remember marching for so long one night that my friend and squadmate, Itamar, actually fell asleep while walking with fifty pounds on his back. I had to hold his hand to make sure that he didn't fall over every time his eyes shut. These weeks in the field ingrained in us the sort of dedication, energy, and focus that might one day be required in those moments in which we were called upon to defend our citizens.

*During a particularly cold, wet,
and difficult week training in the field.*

You never get comfortable (at least I didn't!)
jumping out of a perfectly good plane

The army was a transformative experience for me on a personal level as well. When I began my service, I naively thought I knew what exhaustion, hard work, sacrifice, and commitment were. I was wrong. I also thought I liked tuna. After an entire week of eating nothing but canned tuna for breakfast, lunch, and dinner, I learned that I'd been wrong about that as well. Regardless, I came back to New York more mature, more thankful for my family and friends, and ready to continue along the path I had always been so eager to travel down.

My Role at Drucker Wealth Management

Having been immersed in the family business growing up, I had always dreamed of one day joining the firm that my grandpa had started. My motivation always came back to one reality. My dad had grown his business by taking care of family and friends—helping them to achieve their financial goals and growing with them over time. I thought that was an incredible way to live...doing well by doing good. I still felt that way upon my return from the military, and so I officially made the decision that I had been preparing for almost since I could talk; I dove headfirst into our business. So, what does that mean exactly? What is my role?

Every day, I sit face-to-face with young people, ensuring that they are taking positive steps as they begin their financial journey. Any young professional who is:

- Focused on becoming financially successful,
- Willing to do what it takes to get there, and
- Open to committing to a savings plan, no matter how small...

...is someone I want in my world.

But here's the not-so-secret reality: not many financial advisors are eager to work with members of our generation. It makes sense when you think about it, as we don't have very much money to invest! Case in point, most of my clients are not walking into our next meeting with $5 million available to create a financial plan! So naturally, for most advisors, our generation is not worth the effort yet. But as a multigenerational firm, the Drucker Wealth team—and I, in particular—can afford to think differently.

This is not just a temporary job for me or a phase in my career; this is my life and my legacy (I promise, I get less corny throughout the book!). Simply put, I'm not going anywhere. Being part of a firm that spans three generations and that is established and credentialed, has been around for sixty years, and is committed to the next sixty years has given my young clients and me a rare opportunity to start working together when we're young and building our personal financial foundations. I'm in a position to think not just about what I can do for my clients next week or next month, but also how to best set them up so that we can be successful together five, ten, and twenty years from now. This is huge because as you'll see in each chapter that follows, the earlier we can get started on planning, saving, and building, the better shape we will be in down the road.

So what did diving into the business mean for me? Well, for one, I immediately started preparing to become a Certified Financial Planner, or CFP®, the most highly recognized designation in our industry. To become a Certified Financial Planner, I had to meet the board's rigorous educational requirements (passing six graduate-level courses in the process) before completing a comprehensive board exam. All that craziness is behind me, thankfully, as I earned my CFP® certification in 2018, and in only eleven months instead

of the normal two to three years. As my whole family can tell you, I can be an obsessive nerd about things (I'm going to try really hard not to go on a *Harry Potter* or *Game of Thrones* rant at any point throughout this book), and this was just one of those rare times when it actually worked in my favor. That said, part of my motivation to speed through the program was that I never wanted to be just another person out there calling myself a "financial advisor," a label that practically anyone can attach to his or her name. I wanted *to actually be* a trusted advisor and expert to my growing clientele. It may sound corny, but when you're helping people plan their lives, it's no joke!

Many late nights, early mornings,
and weekends to attain this CFP® designation!

Now, four years into my career, I am incredibly fortunate to be the managing director of Drucker Wealth Builder, our division specially designed to help H.E.N.R.Y.s, so that together we can start planning for our generation's future. Our whole mission is to help our young clients transition from their current standing as H.E.N.R.Y.s toward their rightful place as empowered adults on the path to financial success (sorry, despite my best efforts, there wasn't an acronym that fit there!).

What Exactly Is a H.E.N.R.Y.?

I want to spend a moment here reflecting on what a H.E.N.R.Y. is because it's an idea that has resonated so feverishly with all of the young professionals to whom I'm introduced (and it's the title of the book, after all) that It's actually given many of them a new and optimistic perspective as they prepare themselves for the financial choices and challenges that await them.

A H.E.N.R.Y. is a young professional making a healthy salary and living what kids today would call their "best life." If you're a H.E.N.R.Y., you may be able to eat out, travel a few times a year, go to the gym and workout classes of your choosing, and attend events and concerts more or less with no worries, but you're still living with one or two roommates. You don't think twice about buying drinks at the bar (being four drinks in already doesn't hurt), but you're still not saving enough into your 401(k) or your savings account. Simply put, you're in good shape right now earning a great salary, and, even without thinking about your finances, you'll actually continue being OK for a while as you make and spend money each month.

At the same time, you're not actually planning, saving, or building in a way that allows you to even think about buying that first home, starting a family, changing careers, or doing any of the other exciting things you have in mind for your future. A H.E.N.R.Y. with no plans on graduating from that title is simply living day to day, without making the sort of active decisions in their financial life that are going to change their financial situation in any substantial way. In other words, A H.E.N.R.Y. is basically running in place. That's OK though. The beauty in being a H.E.N.R.Y. is that we're not rich…yet.

This definition of a H.E.N.R.Y. is actually a question I actually get asked all the time…

So you might be asking at this point, well, "How much money do I need to make to be a H.E.N.R.Y?" Or, "Is there a maximum net worth I can have and still be considered a H.E.N.R.Y?" My answer is always the same: it's not about the numbers. I work with H.E.N.R.Y.'s who make $100,00 annually and those who make a few million. Being a H.E.N.R.Y. is not about having a particular income or a specific numerical net worth, but rather, that feeling in your gut that you could be doing MORE; you could be planning and preparing with more purpose if only you knew what that entailed.

Part of why I created this concept of fighting H.E.N.R.Y. Syndrome® is because it's a descriptor that you can't necessarily define, but if it describes your situation, it hits you like a ton of bricks! I do a lot of speaking to young professional groups around New York City and every so often, I'll describe (in excruciating detail) what being a H.E.N.R.Y. "feels" like and someone will scream out, "OMG that's me!!!" And they blurt it out almost accidentally or instinctually because they're so caught up in the moment, amazed at how perfectly this H.E.N.R.Y. idea describes their life and their feelings about money.

Anecdotally, this realization is the best thing that could happen to their financial future. It can become a catalyst for change. When people intuitively sense that this "syndrome" defines how they've been living, two things happen. One, you know that there must be steps out there that you can take to "cure" the syndrome (in a manner of speaking) and find yourself in a better financial situation. Taking that first step and becoming more educated and empowered with regards to your financial situation is always a good thing; knowledge is power. Equally as important, it removes that guilt or embarrassment of not having gotten started down the financial planning path already! It allows you to realize that you're not alone: there are millions of H.E.N.R.Y.'s out there that share those same financial anxieties that you do and, most crucially, it's not too late to get started!

At DWM, we trademarked the term H.E.N.R.Y. Syndrome and built an entire division of our firm around the idea precisely because there is still time for most young professionals to get there. Our Wealth Builder division, and my focus, is about bridging that gap and starting young professionals on that path toward the ultimate achievement of their financial goals.

> Our Wealth Builder division, and my focus, is about bridging that gap and starting young professionals on that path toward the ultimate achievement of their financial goals.

My Goal for This Book

So why did I write a book? And why now?

As I embark on planning for my own financial future as well as planning the futures of my clients who are similar in age as me, I wanted to build and organize my ark of lessons

23

and stories that might help all of us better navigate the financial choices we make and the crossroads where we'll often find ourselves as we get older. I want to offer real strategies to make our financial decisions more manageable. As to why I'm sharing this now, so early in my career, is the simple reality that these ideas aren't just relevant for my clients but for myself as well...I'm twenty-eight years old at the time of writing this book! I understand the challenges, dilemmas, and yes, opportunities, in starting to plan for your future because I'm living and breathing everything that I'm writing. This is as much my journey as it is yours. As such, this is my first collection of these thoughts, but as I move further down life's winding road, I'm certain they won't be the last!

Everything you'll read in this book will be in plain English—no fancy acronyms, confusing jargon, or secret codes here. This isn't about rating this-or-that fund's standard deviation or best practices while using the Monte Carlo simulation. In fact, I think I almost blacked out while writing that sentence; suffice it to say I have zero interest in trying to write (or even read) paragraphs on those aspects of finance. This is also definitely not a book that will advise you which stock to pick or which way the market will move next Tuesday at three o'clock in the afternoon, because I have no idea, and really, nobody else does either (as we'll see in a later chapter).

These pages are devoted to big-picture ideas, lessons, and relevant anecdotes about personal money management, financial goal planning, retirement planning, investment management, and protection planning. I've crafted these ideas through my evolving experiences as a financial advisor and public speaker to the young professional world, and I promise you only one thing: each story and idea will make you think about what you're doing in your own financial life!

2

The Only Number
that Matters

*"Money, it turned out, was exactly like sex, you
thought of nothing else if you didn't have it and
thought of other things if you did."*
–James Arthur Baldwin

Let's start off with a question. If you had to define your current financial situation using only one figure, what number would be the best gauge of how you're doing? I'm sure your first thought was your annual salary or your net worth, right? That's what I hear most often when people begin to explain their financial life to me.

However, without a doubt, the most important number—and really, the *only* number—that matters at this point in your career, is how much you're able to save each year. That's it. Because as we get older, it's never about how much money we make; it's about how much of that income we can actually get to keep. This truth will become the driving force in our quest to become financially independent.

> The most important number that matters at this point in your career is how much you're able to save each year.

Actually, hold on. We just threw out a big idea—"financial independence"—and I don't want us to get ahead of ourselves here.

What Does Financial Independence Mean?

Building a road map to financial independence is what this book is all about. We want to be clear on what it is we're shooting for, so let's pause for a moment and discuss what "wealth" and "financial independence" mean from the standpoint of how becoming so would affect our lives. Being financially independent, to me, means getting to a point at which I can make choices for my family and myself without being dependent upon the mercy of my paycheck to support these

> Financial independence means not *needing* a paycheck to support your living costs

choices. Put another way—financial independence means not *needing* a paycheck to support your living costs, because your accumulated assets, rather than the sweat of your brow, can provide a stable income for you and your family for life.

If you're fortunate enough to reach this level of success, retirement occurs when you *choose* to step off the wheel, not just when you can afford to do so. This is a lofty goal, no doubt, and most Americans never get there. In fact, a lot of millionaires never get there. But when we

look at the most successful people in our extended social circles, those who are truly wealthy and without financial worries, isn't this what we're describing? Freedom. The freedom to live a life of our own choosing. Isn't this what we're striving for? Why not dream big?

Photo by Oliver Sjöström on Unsplash

But that's for later. For now, let's get back to our discussion about the most important number in our financial universe: the amount we're able to save!

Making Money versus Keeping Money

If every dollar you make is going back out, i.e., being spent, then you're not really building any sort of wealth over time. Think about it: if you're making a ridiculous amount of money, but you're spending it all, what's really happening? You may be eating really well (still not an acceptable reason to Instagram your meals, as far as I'm concerned), you may get to run up a ridiculous bar tab that you don't even remember the next morning, and you may have some really cool toys, but you're not actually building wealth as we've just defined it.

Now, you may be thinking to yourself that everything I just described sounds pretty good, and being able to live that lifestyle is exactly why you're working so hard; that's fine! Eating well, traveling frequently, and having nice things can be really exciting and even comforting, and I'm certainly not trying to downplay that, because the truth is, we all have different motivations that drive us.

But living this way, unfortunately, does not actually get you closer to becoming wealthy, retiring early, sending your kids to the best schools, or buying that dream beach house for your family. You're just spinning on that income wheel, never able to hop off without immediately losing your balance and falling over.

Image provided by Dreamstime / ID 29690969 © Aleutie | Dreamstime.com

As you grow accustomed to spending more and more money, you will remain wholly dependent on that high income to maintain your lifestyle forever, with no real assets accumulated to show for all of your hard work. It's the equivalent of someone trying to get in really great shape for beach season by working out and training like an animal (metaphorically, making a lot of money), but then they're gorging on McDonald's every night right before bed (spending it all). The workouts don't matter so much after a week of eating Big Macs and fries! It's the same idea here: spending all of your hard-earned money doesn't put you in a position to build wealth. Let's take it even one step further. Beyond being unable to save money with these types of spending habits, can you imagine what would happen to you if that income, for whatever reason, were to disappear or even dip a little? Absolute chaos! I don't even want to imagine living with such poor spending habits and income stress dictating my life.

The Danger of Lifestyle Creep

OK, *smart guy*, you're saying to yourself, *well then, what's the alternative? How do we avoid this trap?* We're getting there...but first, let's dig deeper into this idea that our income and our spending are attached at the hip (even if it's unintentional), with each of them rising together over time.

This situation of never truly becoming financially independent or building your net worth despite continuing to make more money every year is more common than you might think. On some level, it doesn't make sense. As you make more money, doesn't that mean that you'll naturally have a lot more to store away? Unfortunately, not. We see it all too often as advisors—people think that because they're *making* more money each year, they can *spend* more money each year! This phenomenon is called lifestyle creep. The truth is that people feel like they need to keep purchasing a bigger home, driving nicer cars, going on more extravagant vacations, and buying nicer watches, purses, clothes, and the like simply because they can. It's almost as if they can't imagine not making these types of lifestyle enhancements despite knowing that only a few short years ago,

> People think that because they're *making* more money each year, they have to *spend* more money each year! This phenomenon is called lifestyle creep.

they couldn't afford to live this way, and they were still completely OK!

That's why I think "creep" is such a great word for this behavior. It's not always a conversation—or even a conscious decision—that you're going to spend to your upper limit now that you make more money, but rather the behavior becomes ingrained in you as the spending increases gradually from year to year. Then you wake up one day, and your income ceases to be a way for you to become financially independent, and instead, just a means for you to accumulate more stuff and spend more extravagantly.

If you've ever seen *Talladega Nights* with Will Ferrell (comedic gold, as far as I'm concerned), there's a scene right after Will Ferrell's simpleton character gets famous overnight (after he wins a big NASCAR race) that always gets me. As he's being interviewed on national television, his hands keep awkwardly raising higher and higher close to his face before he uncomfortably tells the interviewer, "I don't know what to do with my hands." The interviewer pushes Ferrell's hands down to help, but somehow 30 seconds later, Will's character is raising them again as he's answering another interview question. It's a ridiculous scene…but I always think about it in connection with lifestyle creep. Will Ferrell's hands are exactly like the spending habits of way too many Americans! Our spending just keeps rising and rising unintentionally and unwittingly until one day until you're forced to tell someone, "I don't know what to do about my spending."

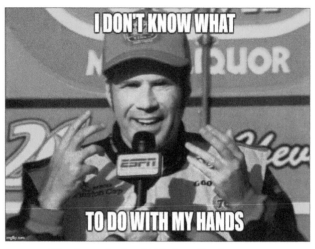

*The first of a few Will Ferrell references
in this book...be warned!*

Dan and Linda's (Increased!) Spending

I saw this firsthand in one of the very first meetings that I sat in on at my dad's office. The meeting hammered into my brain that lifestyle creep was a real thing—because before, it just seemed kind of ridiculous and theoretical, as it might to you. *C'mon,* I thought, *as someone makes more money, they'll inevitably save more money.* How wrong I was. Anyway, we were meeting with Dan and Linda, a husband and wife who were in our office for the first time. They were both attorneys, each making great six-figure salaries, and had come in to see us at the recommendation of their friend, who was a client of ours. Their only real motivation for doing so was because Dan had moved firms and had a retirement account at a previous firm, and he wanted our help in managing the money. That was it. They really didn't see themselves as needing any "financial planning help;" as far as they knew, they had everything covered.

We went through some preliminary questions, and Dan mentioned that they each made $500,000 to $600,000 annually, and had been making about that much for over a decade. To be honest, upon hearing that, I expected their net worth to be incredibly impressive. After all, they were making over $1 million annually and had been for some time. But when we got down to learning about their assets, we found that really wasn't the case. Don't get me wrong; they were fine and were still doing better than most people walking down the street. This isn't a sob story! But their net worth was nowhere close to the level of wealth I would have guessed only fifteen minutes earlier. When our new clients left, I asked my dad if he was surprised by the lack of money in their savings accounts, investment accounts, etc. He shrugged.

"Nope. They live in a really expensive area, they drive nice cars, their kids go to private school, and there's no real plan driving their savings behavior. They've been just gliding by. It kind of makes sense."

Looking back, I believe that was truly one of the best meetings I've ever sat in on because I saw the power and the struggle of "lifestyle creep" up close. We eventually did a comprehensive Financial Life Plan (discussed in Chapter 5) with them that revealed that unless they immediately started changing their behavior, they would both have to work until they were ninety years old. They've since adjusted some of their spending, and toned down some of their more extravagant habits, and they're committed to saving the set number that we outlined together. But the results were shocking to them. They didn't feel like they were spending so much money; it was almost as if their monthly spending had crept up on them! (In case you're wondering, yup, I was winking as I wrote that last line.)

Jake's Wake Up Call

Luckily for my clients and the young people reading this book, we can stop this "creep" from shooting us in the foot *before* it gets to an overwhelming point in our fifties. In fact, I remember doing just that with one of my clients, Jake, two years ago. Jake, a well-paid software engineer in his late twenties, was coming into my office for one of our first meetings, and he was excited to get to work figuring out exactly what he had made, spent, saved, etc., over the preceding year. Jake liked to dine out and travel a lot (although he blamed it on his girlfriend, I knew it was equally his own doing), and as a result, it turned out that his annual savings was only about 10 percent of his income.

Important note: Throughout this whole chapter, when I say "savings" I don't mean necessarily a "savings" account, I'm just referring to saving money any way you can...that could mean to bank accounts, brokerage investment accounts, retirement accounts like your 401(k), etc. We're not up to "where" the money should be saved, that breakdown will come later, for now, we're just focused on the breakdown between money being saved and the money that's spent.

As for Jake, in that first meeting, he wasn't the slightest bit worried about his saving habits because, he told me, "I'll make the same amount next year and will probably even be getting a raise," and his checking account was going up every month, so he was saving *some* money. Everything was fine!

At that point, I took out a marker and wrote on the whiteboard in my office how much money he had made in the last five years, and I added it up to determine the total. It was a huge number, and he was understandably excited, just seeing it laid out like that. Then, in the next column, I wrote out his resulting net worth at the end of each year. The year-to-year change was, shall we say, lower. He grew quiet. I imagine he was thinking back to all those late nights at the office, weekends spent fixing code, and all of the three o'clock in the morning email exchanges with clients and bosses that he had endured to earn all of that money. It took him a minute, but then it hit him: he was never getting that money back! The funds for that first house he wanted to buy in three years or the engagement ring he was hoping to get for his girlfriend, all of that income (the number I had first written down) was gone. It was, at this point, a meaningless number! He had already made and spent that money.

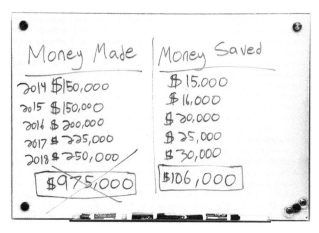

The drawing that helped my client see the light.

In the three years since that first meeting, his income was never a talking point again. He was only focused on how much he had saved each and every year, and that became the focus of all of our planning moving forward. As luck would have it, his net worth began to grow exponentially after his mental shift from caring about how much he made to how much he was able to save. How we were able to build a program for him to start saving money, and the strategies we put in place to ensure that it continued into the future is a story for a later chapter, but for now, my point is simply that the mindset needs to change first. Once this occurs, it's almost impossible to go back to thinking in the old income-driven way—the one in which you're motivated primarily by your salary and how much you can spend rather than the amount of money that's actually staying in your pocket!

What Are Our Twenties & Thirties For?

So, you may be thinking, OK, *but Jake was in his late twenties; he was* supposed *to be eating out, traveling, and having great experiences! It was his first time really making money, so why not?!* You're right. I absolutely understand that way of thinking, and I even agree to a certain extent. Being young and without much responsibility is the time to have fun and gain as much life experience as you can. I'm twenty-eight years old—of course I get this!

I'm not at all saying that immediately upon making money, you should be stashing away every single dollar and eating nothing but canned food or a cup of soup every night. But I also know that thinking about saving for the future even just *a little bit* when you're young and have decades ahead of you can go a long way toward the ultimate fulfillment of your financial dreams.

Like with anything else, there needs to be a balance between enjoying life and building for the future, and that balance looks a little bit different for each person we sit down with. Part of our role is to help you strike the perfect balance for *you*. Before we get there though, we need first to show you *why* it's so important to start saving money when you're young. How do we do that? Well, using the actual dollars available to you at the moment of our meeting, we'll illustrate what saving even marginally more money today will mean for your ability to achieve tomorrow's dreams.

It's a powerful thing to be able to see for yourself what you can start doing right away, with the money you're actually making, and how even those small shifts can translate to more significant and dramatic changes down the road. When you attach real numbers to your goals and understand the tangible benefits of starting early, "saving money" becomes less hypothetical or intimidating, and the future doesn't seem quite as impossibly far away.

Consider this the first step of that conversation: motivating you to get excited about saving money for your future. Let's discuss, using a real life (kind of) example to articulate why saving money when you're young and just getting started in the workplace is like adding jet fuel to your financial future.

My family is obsessed with the movie *Step Brothers*. While I'm not sure exactly what that says about the Drucker clan, I need my charts to stay true to character! But beyond just making you consider which "Step Brother" would have been better at saving money, I want you to see the true power of starting to save when you're young. As the chart on the next page makes clear, Brennan is able to accumulate more money than his brother, Dale, despite saving less money and for a much shorter period of time, simply because he let the beauty of time and compound interest work in his favor! I'll also point out that for each brother, we're showing an annual savings of only $1,000...that's less than $100 month! So, this isn't a ridiculous example in which you would need to be saving six figures each year in order for the point to hit home. When discussing the power of saving money, I always prefer to use smaller numbers because it illustrates the reality that every dollar, you're putting away now will go a long way toward the compounding growth of your net worth.

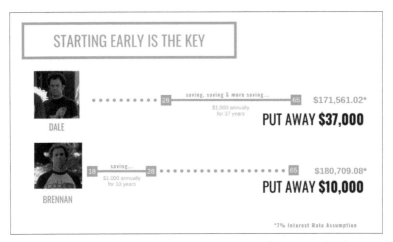

Brennan had to save a lot less money for a much shorter period of time, and yet he still wound up with the larger account simply because he let the power of time work in his favor. Simply put, by starting a decade earlier, because of the power of compound interest, Brennan had much more potential for his money to compound over time.

Friends, this isn't rocket science. Of course, the younger you are when you start planning for the future and putting away money, all else being equal, the better off you're going to be; there will be more years in which you're stashing away money! This is obvious…but this actually wasn't what just happened in our Step Brothers example…check it out again. We intentionally had Brennan save less money (and for less time) and still wind up on top to illustrate the powerful effects of compounding interest over time when you're young. The reason Brennan finished with more money than his brother is that all of the money he saved in those first ten years had more time to grow and compound on its own, like a boulder gaining more momentum as it barrels down a hill, before Dale had even started saving. In other words, his money was already picking up steam (compounding on itself) by the time Dale started, and it was impossible for Dale's money to gain enough momentum to catch up later on.

Compound interest means that you're earning interest each year on the principal amount you started with AND the accumulated interest that you've already earned in prior years. In other words, your interest starts earning interest! Can you see how time really is the most important asset we have given that this is how money grows over time? Let's use an even simpler analogy to drive the point home:

A Single Penny Doubled Everyday

Day 1	$.01		Day 16	$327.68
Day 2	$.02		Day 17	$655.36
Day 3	$.04		Day 18	$1,310.72
Day 4	$.08		Day 19	$2,621.44
Day 5	$.16		Day 20	$5,242.88
Day 6	$.32		Day 21	$10,485.76
Day 7	$.64		Day 22	$20,971.52
Day 8	$1.28		Day 23	$41,943.04
Day 9	$2.56		Day 24	$83,886.08
Day 10	$5.12		Day 25	$167,772.16
Day 11	$10.24		Day 26	$335,544.32
Day 12	$20.48		Day 27	$671,088.64
Day 13	$40.96		Day 28	$1,342,177.28
Day 14	$81.92		Day 29	$2,684,354.56
Day 15	$163.84		Day 30	$5,368,709.12

As you can see in the graph above, it's the last three days in which the bulk of your money compounds. If your money was invested for only ten days, then this would have been a ridiculous exercise and the answer would have been obvious (take the five million!). Conversely, if we extended the daily doubling by an extra few weeks, we'd be talking about you having Mark Cuban money! The point is not that your money is going to double every day (of course not!!), but that money needs time for you to truly realize the benefits of compounding interest. This ultimately gets back to our point that the more money you're able to stash away when you're young, the better off you're going to be, if no other reason than you have time on your side.

To wrap up this idea, think about it like this: there are two ways to make money. People can make money (via jobs), and money can make money (via investing). But we can't even discuss how to invest your into vehicles that can grow if there's no money left each month to save in the first place. We'll get into what this means from an investment allocation standpoint later on, but the biggest takeaway for now should be that the only way we have money for compounding interest to work its beautiful magic is to save (and not spend) our hard earned money!!

> There are two ways to make money. People can make money (via jobs), and money can make money (via investing).

Sarah Asks My Favorite Question

I had another new client, Sarah, a twenty-eight-year-old in marketing, come in one day to meet with me for the first time. After giving me a better sense of her financial situation, she asked me the question that had clearly been on her mind throughout the entire meeting: In my opinion, how did she financially compare to some of my other clients? I knew it was coming. This is the most frequent question I'm asked in a first meeting, especially by people in their twenties and thirties who come to me without any sort of concrete financial plan. They'll ask a version of Sarah's question: "Is this about how much I should have saved at this point based on what you've seen?"

I get it. I really do. I understand the human impulse to compare, but it's an utterly meaningless exercise. I think young people are so obsessed with comparing themselves to their roommates, colleagues, girlfriends, brothers-in-law, et al. because it's the only way to see any kind of snapshot of how they're doing, without actually putting in the work of creating their own road map and understanding how they're doing relative to accomplishing their own goals. Believing that you're doing "better" than Sally up the street can make you feel temporarily relieved about not having a specific plan or knowing where you stand, but in reality, Sally and you have totally different goals, means, and financial journeys ahead of you.

Put another way, Sally may actually be closer to achieving her goals than you are despite your higher net worth because she's not planning for graduate school, or she has a retirement pension, or she spends less each month, or whatever—who knows! And that's kind of the point. It sounds cliché, but we should only be concerned with how we stack up relative to our *own* goals, dreams, and liabilities. In fact, the few clients who come to me with an actual financial plan—with their goals, budget, and time horizon properly laid out—never seem to ask about Joe down the block because they are confident in knowing what they have to do to achieve their own goals and are only concerned with the practical steps to get there.

Image provided by Dreamstime / ID 49537058 © Blueringmedia | Dreamstime.com

The Saver versus the Banker

In case you were wondering, yes, it did feel great to get that off my chest! But let's get back to Sarah's question. She was worried that she didn't make enough, and the truth was, in a sense, she was right. Because of Sarah's chosen industry, she was making less than other people her age, including her roommates (a fact that understandably caused her some anxiety.) Then I shared with her the good news: despite her making less money than some of her peers, she was actually a lot further along the path to her goal of buying her first home, starting a family, and investing for the future. Why? Because she was disciplined as hell! She was conscientious about how much she spent and she valued the money she was earning. And after looking at the plan we'd put together, she determined that she was capable of putting away 25 percent of her income each year.

Translation: She's living below her means and saving a *disproportionate amount of money* each month for her future. This is, without question, the single greatest determinant as to whether or not she will achieve her financial goals.

Evaluating your financial picture by the amount you're able to save rather than by how much you make is the first step to seeing the light!

A banker who is making double the amount of Sarah's income but only saving 10 percent of his salary (I see it all too often) is actually in worse shape if we define "better" as being closer to financial independence and accumulating wealth over time. Put more simply, which one of them is

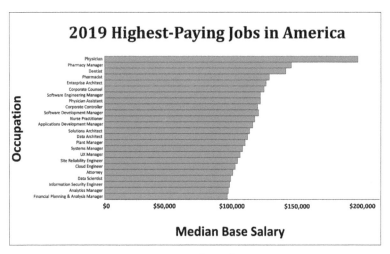

Your income earning potential, as shown, is important...
but so is your ability to save it![2]

going to increase his or her account balances in the next ten years: the saver or the banker who is hardly saving?

Now, saving more money isn't an easy habit to start, and without an actionable plan, it's definitely not easy to continue. We will dive deeper into this later on, but for now, the biggest takeaway is this: evaluating your financial picture by the amount you're able to save rather than by how much you make is the first step to seeing the light!

3

Live Below Your Means

*"Money isn't the most important thing in life,
but it's reasonably close to oxygen
on the 'gotta have it' scale."*
–Zig Ziglar

My grandpa Bernie was a self-made man. His family, like many immigrant families, didn't have much money. Making it even tougher on him, his father passed away when Bernie was only sixteen, and his brother was away fighting in World War II, leaving Bernie, a high school student, as the man of the house. He was responsible for taking care of his mom and younger sisters. From this early life experience, he developed one goal that guided his decision-making for the rest of his life: to make his family and himself financially independent.

Every decision that he and his wife, my grandma, made was geared toward taking care of their family and getting to a point in life where they weren't at the mercy of a paycheck. Simply put, he wanted to get to a position later in life in which he could relax because he had never been able to do so as a young man. This mission manifested itself in his approach to spending money.

Poppy Bernie's Vision

My grandpa lived well below his means. My grandparents, dad, and Aunt Dawn lived in a modest home in a blue-collar suburb on Long Island. My dad and aunt went to day camp instead of sleepaway camp, maintained summer jobs throughout high school, and attended state colleges instead of private universities. Of course, nobody should feel bad for my dad and aunt; that's not the point of the story. They had a traditional middle-class American life. What matters is that my grandpa made certain choices, most of them of the day-to-day-spending variety and not as significant as those I've mentioned previously. However, every single choice he made was intentional and aligned with his singular goal of achieving financial independence. Quite simply, these decisions added up. Sure, at his income level, they absolutely could have lived in a bigger home, or gone on more extravagant vacations, had nicer cars, and stretched their spending more, but my grandpa had a vision that he would not stray from until he'd achieved it.

Just as he is mine, my dad's hero was always his dad Bernie. Here's the two of them outside their home in East Meadow, Long Island.

An Artificial Environment of Economic Scarcity

My grandpa saved a disproportionate amount of his income; unlike most Americans, he spent nowhere near his upper limit. He once told my dad that he "created for himself an artificial environment of economic scarcity," a brilliant idea that he took from *The Millionaire Next Door*, one of the most important books that I've ever read (more on that at the end of this chapter). Simply put, my grandpa acted like he had a lot less money to spend than he really did so that he would live below his means and automatically save the rest. My grandpa was resolute that he would save 25 percent of his gross income, and he would have to make do with living on the rest. In other words, he pretended he made only 75 percent of the money than he actually did. The money that he put away would be saved and allocated for the future; he would not touch it for any short-term expenditures.

> Consider this: whatever money you put away is to be saved and allocated for the future; do not touch it for any short-term expenditures.

I would reread those last few lines again because there's a simple beauty to what my grandpa did that ensured, absolutely *ensured*, that he would never become a victim of his own success or his own income. Even as he continued to make more money, he never veered from that plan to save at least 25 percent of his income each month, and to do so first. For my grandpa, earning a higher income allowed him to save more—and then, and only then, spend more generously as he was able to. But he would never find himself in

Dan and Linda's situation, one in which spending got out of control and they became servants to their own income. My grandpa ultimately achieved that financial success he dreamed of—he lived out his days with no financial worries and he was able to retire comfortably. On top of that, he left a legacy of love for his entire family and changed his family's financial future through the lessons he passed down.

Numbers Change; Values Don't

Growing up with his father, Bernie, as his role model, my dad learned at a young age the value of a dollar and the importance of saving money. At age sixteen, when he began working, my dad immediately started saving his designated percentage, even if the amount he saved back then was more symbolic than anything else. Fast-forward thirty-five years, and he has reached his goal of becoming financially independent. Part of the reason why he has done so well for himself over the years is that he has never subscribed to the idea that you have to spend your money or show it off just because you can. In other words, his values didn't change just because he started making more money as he got older.

The things that were important to him to spend his money on at age thirty-five (his family, self-improvement, and his passions) didn't change at fifty-five just because he was operating with larger numbers. My dad has always valued experiences and anything to do with his family over mate-rial possessions. He has enjoyed spending money on things like basketball coaches, personal trainers, tennis camps, and Krav Maga lessons for his family; sending donations to the causes he's passionate about; being able to travel when he wants to (including visiting me in Israel every few months while I was there); and choosing camps and universities that were the best fit for my sister, Gabby, and me. I feel beyond fortunate, not just for the opportunities his success allowed for us while growing up, but also for the values and discipline that his example provided as we started down our own path.

My Sister, the Saving Rock Star

I need to take a moment and comment on how much my sister drank the Kool-Aid. She's a machine. Gabby is a personal trainer and small-business owner in Philadelphia, and she is getting started on building out her empire: Drucker

My sister Gabby leading her students through a 'Drucker Fitness' style workout!

Fitness. The second edition of this book may be a combination of fitness and finance and be co-authored by the two of us, so be on the lookout for it!

Gabby teaches group workout classes and runs individual training sessions in her apartment building, at various training studios around the city, and sometimes even outside, taking advantage of literally every hour in the day. She'll teach on a Saturday morning and a Sunday night, and sometimes has eleven sessions in a day. What's even more amazing than how hard she works is how diligent she is about saving her money. She has, more than any other client I've met with, that "saver" mentality of living below her means and making sure she's saving a disproportionate amount of her income each month. Of course, given our upbringing, this isn't surprising to me in the slightest!

In order to save money, Gabby practices all of the following activities:

- Cooks and plans out her meals for the week ahead of time and rarely eats out on weekdays
- Makes coffee every morning and then puts the rest on ice, so she has iced coffee to bring to work (no Starbucks coffee for her!)
- Prides herself on having lived with her husband in a smaller apartment than they were originally interested in, in order to build up a joint cash cushion
- Drinks mostly water throughout the day and always from her refillable bottle

- Walks and takes the train instead of driving, as often as she can

My point in sharing some of the choices that Gabby has made is not that they are the most important life changes that one could possibly make. In fact, my point is the exact opposite! None of these are life-altering or even inconvenient choices. They do not impede on my sister's ability to have fun and do the things she wants to do. But, because Gabby has an awareness of the importance of saving and building wealth, she's able to see these small opportunities for what they are, and she can spend money guilt-free on the things she truly cares about!

The Millionaire Next Door

Previously, I mentioned the book, *The Millionaire Next Door*, and I want to convey a few takeaways before you go out and buy your own copy, because its lessons were truly life-changing for me. The authors, Thomas J. Stanley and

William D. Danko, set out to discover which characteristics are shared by America's millionaires: What do they look like? Where do they live? What type of cars do they drive? What do they do for a living? The results were staggering.

Because we all tend to associate investment bankers, attorneys, athletes, and the like with incredible wealth, the number of America's millionaires who are actually small-business owners, teachers, corporate middle management, "regular" professionals, and others might astound you. Most of these millionaires had middle-of-the-pack salaries. In fact, you would never have guessed that most of them were millionaires if you'd just looked at how much money they made (see Chapter 2). The most eye-opening part of their stories, however, was what united most of

> America's millionaires live *well* below their means... they are making average, middle-class salaries that would never assume could be the salaries of the affluent.

these men and women. There was one behavior, more than any other unifying characteristic, that repeatedly revealed itself throughout the authors' quest: the overwhelming percentage of America's millionaires live *well* below their means. They weren't wearing, driving, or living in their wealth, but rather, had stored it away relentlessly each and every year.

Again, because I don't think it can be repeated enough, a high percentage of these millionaires were making average, middle-class salaries that you would never assume could be the salaries of the affluent. But like my grandpa, they had a vision, a plan, and lived a lifestyle that allowed them to achieve their financial goals. My greatest takeaway from the book was that we have way more control and power over our financial future than we might ordinarily think. It's up to us how we choose to live.

Of course, we all have different things that drive us. My grandpa's (and my dad's) way isn't the *only* way or even necessarily the *right* way. I can't make the decision for you about what you value. But if becoming financially independent is a goal of yours, if becoming wealthy and creating a legacy for your family is a part of your life's mission, then living below your means is the surest way to get there.

4

Pay Yourself First

*"Budget: a mathematical confirmation
of your suspicions."*
–A.A. Latimer

So, beginning to mentally value the amount of money you're able to save rather than just caring about your salary is great and all, but saving more money isn't just going to occur by osmosis; there needs to be a plan of attack.

Sam's End of the Month Strategy

My client Sam realized this in one of our first meetings together, three years ago. I was asking Sam about his current budget, investment portfolio, cash flow, and protection plan when we got down to the most important part of the conversation: How much was he saving each month? He explained that his "system" was to add whatever's leftover in his checking account at the end of the month (after paying bills, rent, groceries, etc.) to his savings account. (This is how most people I meet with do things, even those who are disciplined and well intentioned.) The amount in his savings account generally increased each month, and so he never thought to question the numbers; increases are good, and that was enough for him! But when we got down to brass tacks, he realized that for all the great money he was making, he really wasn't putting away as much as he had thought. This uncomfortable fact was staring him right in the face.

After a moment of heavy silence, a dejected expression settled upon Sam's face.

He shrugged his shoulders and remarked, "I guess it is what it is. That's how much is left," before trailing off.

That was my opportunity to step in and ask him a question I remembered having overheard my dad ask a client's son when I was first starting out: "What would you do if your rent went up by $500 a month? Would you move?"

Sam thought about it for a second before definitively answering, "No way. I love my apartment and moving in New York City is the worst. I'd figure out a way to make it work. I'd cut back some of my stupid spending."

"OK," I said, "what if it went up by $700?"

He gave me the same answer. Eventually, we got to a number at which he would have to think about moving. It was over $900.

I said, "Great! So we *know* that you can save at least another $900 if you want to. Awesome!"

My point was that he actually did have *far more* capacity to save than he'd thought possible. It had just never seemed like a priority to him, so he didn't do it. If saving that extra $900 was seen as a necessary expense, if he was forced to allocate that money toward something he deemed important, like staying in his apartment, he could easily have cut his spending each month. We know this with certainty because that $900 he was throwing away on "mindless spending" (his words, not mine!) could have been cobbled together to ensure that he didn't have to move if it came to that. For example (and he admitted as much), he could cook more often instead of ordering delivery most nights, bring his lunch to work, and limit his Amazon purchases to things he really needed.

What Do *You* Prioritize?

So why the difference in attitude? Why did Sam feel tapped out when it came to saving money for his future, but he could have easily adjusted his spending to accommodate an increase in rent? For Sam, rent money was a *necessary expense* that required planning, whereas saving for the future felt like a luxury only permitted if there was any money left over. As a young man, he may have even thought that he had plenty of time to start saving later on in life. But as we learned earlier, this mindset can keep us playing catchup to our own incomes forever.

This is human nature; saving money for an unquantifiable future can seem hypothetical—it may come or it may not—whereas that sizzling steak dinner on Friday is going

Image provided by istoc-Photo / ID 157952934 © gerenme | istockphoto.com

to be delicious right away...we know exactly what it's going to taste like and how it will make us feel. Again, this makes sense. As a society, we want everything immediately; instant gratification—no matter the source—can be addicting. Choosing to defer that happiness, even when we know it's in our best interest is a constant source of friction for most of us.

For this very reason, one of our very first steps when creating a written Financial Life Plan for new clients (see Chapter 5) is to show, using real probabilities, how drastically any extra dollars saved today can improve one's likelihood of success years down the road.

Seeing how those extra saved dollars today will ultimately help pay for your personal and specific goals in the future will help make saving more real and prioritized in the way it should be. It will allow you to see the potential fruits of your labors ahead of time and give you the foresight, motivation, and discipline to defer those dollars (and the gratification that comes with it) to your future.

All of this is to say that if Sam had placed as much emphasis on his ability to save money (which, again, is the single greatest indicator of his family's future financial success), as he did on staying in his apartment, he would have gotten it done. Maybe your number isn't $900. Maybe it's only $300. Cool, that's totally fine! The important thing is to have an approach that maximizes your ability to save money over time without drastically overwhelming your quality of life.

Turning the Corner: What's Next?

Part of my job is to help people figure out a savings strategy that works for them (this is not a "one size fits all" approach). We work together to make saving automatic, easy, and transparent (because left to our own devices, we can be our own worst enemy!), and I help them figure out the best accounts for their savings to reside in order to help them to achieve their goals (a Roth IRA, a savings account, a brokerage portfolio, etc.). But, if you haven't bought in to the idea that saving money should be a prerequisite (and quite frankly, something that excites and empowers you), rather than an "oh, by the way!" on the last day of the month, there's not much we can do that's going to change your financial fortune.

But let's say, upon reading these opening pages, you are now a changed man or woman! You're moments away from slamming the book on the table with authority, running to your kitchen, throwing out that $5 Starbucks coffee that you didn't really need, and declaring for all of your apartment to hear, "Today is the dawn of a new era! Today is the day I'm going to commit to make saving money a priority!" (I'm hoping that at least one person reading this does that…humor me!) So what comes next? How do we actually get there?

Let's deconstruct this idea and figure out our plan moving backward. I'm going to ask you a question that I ask all of the young professionals in the audience at my workshops around New York City: When you first started working, what was the very first account to which you started saving money outside of your existing checking/savings bank accounts, and why was it your first investment vehicle? Asking strangers in NYC an open-ended question can be a daunting exercise, but I *always* get the same answer here.

The Beauty of a 401(k)

For most of us, the answer is our 401(k). In fact, if you've done nothing else in your financial life, if you've paid no mind to your individual planning, I'm willing to bet that the only vehicle that you're saving money for the future into is your 401(k). Why? Well, first off, during your very first week on the job, you probably had someone in your office sit behind you and show you, line by line, how to open your 401(k) plan and how to contribute to it. However much you committed to contribute that first day would continue to be deposited into your 401(k) account each and every month moving forward without any additional action on your part (i.e.: you didn't have to remember three months later to put money into the account). It was easy, automated, consistent, and safe from any self-defeating behavior: it would keep chugging along.

Current Defined Contribution Plan Data Based on 2016 Form 5500 Annual Reports (released December 2018)		
Total Participants	**Active Participants**	**Total Assets***
100.2 million	80.0 million	$5.7 trillion

According to the most recent Federal Reserve data, defined contribution plans comprised total household assets of $6.2 trillion as of the first quarter of 2018.

Here's how many Americans are saving into
a defined contribution plan this year (401(k)'s are one such plan).

Why else is this the first (and maybe the only) investment account your money went into? Well, this money never actually hit your checking account! It was taken out of your paycheck automatically, so you never actually had that money in your possession in the first place. It was like those funds didn't even exist as far as you were concerned. This accomplished two important things. First, it prevented you from spending the money. Those dollars were never sitting in your checking account or your wallet, staring you in the face and telling you that you needed, *desperately needed*, that new pair of pants! Second, after a while, I bet you just kind of forgot that you were even contributing to your 401(k), so you grew comfortable living off your monthly paycheck without those extra dollars. You got used to saving that money each month and to use an idea from earlier, you became accustomed to living like you made less money than you actually did—because that money was never at your disposal to begin with.

Think about it from the opposite perspective. Let's say that you're currently saving $800 month to your 401(k) and have been doing so for a while. But now the 401(k) plan is making a change. From now on, instead of this process being automatic, you'll be given the option to siphon off any dollar amount from that $800 originally earmarked for your 401(k) to be added to your biweekly paycheck and then spent (or saved) as you see fit. What would happen? What if that were the case each and every month? I'd imagine that there would be way too many months in which you were no longer saving that full $800! Maybe you decided to spend $100 one month on a nice dinner, $200 the next month on an extra night out, and $400 the next month on a flight to Florida. Over time, you'd probably be saving at least a little less each month to your 401(k) than that original $800 as you grow more accustomed to life with extra discretionary cash each month! After all, it's human nature to start to rationalize these spending decisions (telling yourself, "I worked a lot of late nights this week!" or "I haven't done anything for *me* lately") and grow comfortable with doing so! Well, as your financial coaches, we want to help you fight against that, and that's what having an automated and consistent savings plan does: it protects us from our worst impulses! We want to replicate as much of that same approach that you take with your 401(k) for the rest of your personal planning and saving—if it ain't broke, why fix it?

Our Wealth Creation Account

Our Wealth Creation Strategy for H.E.N.R.Y.s is our way of ensuring that our young clients have a consistent, automated program—aside from their 401(k)—to save money with purpose.

The idea is relatively simple, as all personal financial strategies should be. Let's say you make $3,000 biweekly (or $6,000 per month). Together, we're going to figure out how much you're able to save (based on your fixed

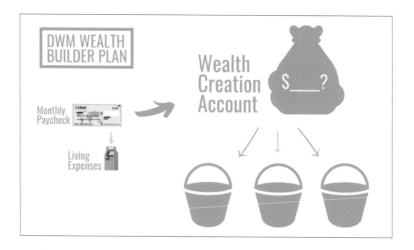

and variable expenses) each month. We determine that your expenses hover between $3,500 and $4,000. Great. We'll call it $4,000 to be safe (any time we start to devise a new strategy for saving money, we want you to be totally comfortable with the amount you're committing to as we can always increase it in the future). We're going to take $1,000 from each paycheck (because you can save $2,000 per month) to fund your future goals. This account will serve as a holding account; the money isn't being invested yet. The entire purpose of this holding account, which we call our Wealth Creation Account (WCA), is that this money is being transferred out of your checking account (which can be easily spent) and into your WCA, which is at least a step removed from your direct access. This is money that you know will be saved each and every month, and as with your 401(k), you won't even be tempted to spend it nor will you have to remember to save it. For some of our clients, creating this WCA and forcing the money out of their hands each month is the most important and calming thing we do for them. They want to know that there's a sound program in place, and for self-employed H.E.N.R.Y.'s or H.E.N.R.Y.'s with bonuses comprising a high percentage of their total income, this is even more crucial! It becomes easy and fulfilling to contribute bonus money, gifts, extra income etc. to the WCA as you grow; ensuring that as you make more (unexpected) income you can immediately allocate it for your future. From there, we will allocate the money from your WCA into your Three Bucket Plan (more on that in Chapter 8), depending on your current financial position and your planning goals moving forward.

We love our Three Bucket Plan. Mostly, because it's a simple way to highlight our fundamental goal of allocating money for specific purposes and their varying time horizons: different buckets for different purposes. This sounds obvious and intuitive—that money should have purpose—but actually it can be a far cry from how people typically think about their money. Often, people we meet will say, "I'm putting money away, and I want it to grow!" Well, that's great, but is that the number one objective for *all* of our money? I don't think so.

For me personally, I know that at various points in my life I'll want some of my money to be safe and accessible, some to provide me with an income stream (through dividends or interest), and some to go to vehicles that are going to protect my other money, assets, and strategies that I employ. There are a number of purposes for why we might save and invest money, and we want to make sure that we're doing so conscientiously! We're going to get more into the bucket plan and the particular investment strategies, vehicles, and programs that come with them in the chapters to come, so I don't want to spend too much time on those subjects now. The point, for now, is that creating a saving strategy that's automated, consistent, and allows you to pay yourself first is one of the very first steps you can take that will allow you to reach your long-term financial goals!

When Student Loans Get in the Way

Before we move on, I want to address an all too common area of financial planning that so many young people with whom I meet have to factor into their expenses and saving plans: student loans! One of the most frequent questions I'm asked at workshops is about student loans, specifically, "Should I pay off my loans or save more money?" Without making light of a great question, my answer is always "Yes."

You might want to read that sentence again; I don't want the joke to get lost on the page!

Quite simply, it's important to do both. Paying down debt (particularly student loans, which can be substantial) is always important, but so, too, is starting to build up your net worth and your emergency fund or cash cushion. I say this for a few reasons.

First off, getting rid of a negative never feels as great as building up a positive. As we discuss frequently throughout this book, the motivations behind our financial behavior and habits (which ultimately dictate our chances for financial success) are usually emotional in nature: how we feel about what we're doing. We want our clients to feel that pride and excitement of seeing their bank accounts grow with time, and we

> Paying down debt (particularly student loans, which can be substantial) is always important, but so, too, is starting to build up your net worth and your emergency fund or cash cushion.

want them to have the peace of mind that comes with knowing that they're building wealth, however slowly, each year. But there's a second and more strictly "financial" reason for ensuring that you're saving money as well as paying down debt. Doing so avoids us falling into a trap.

If you're paying down debt so aggressively that you have very little money saved in an emergency fund as a result, you're putting yourself at risk of going back into more debt at the very next unexpected cost you encounter. If you have minimal savings because every discretionary dollar is going toward paying down your debt, and then your apartment floods (or you switch careers, or you get fired, or you need surgery of some kind, or your car gives out, or your dog gets sick…you get the point) and you have to fall back into credit card debt to pay for (and fix) that new problem, you're just continuing that cycle of debt, unable to ever truly breathe. My dad likes to say achieving financial success with credit card debt is like swimming across the ocean with dumbbells around your neck: possible but a lot tougher than it needs to be. We want to drop the weights.

Student debt, of course, is not the same as credit card debt, and I'm not trying to imply that having student loans is a sign of financial recklessness or of spending too much money when you shouldn't have. For many people, student loans are the cost of having the sort of education and career trajectory that they seek. As long as there's a plan to tackle those student loans, they're not a long-term problem as

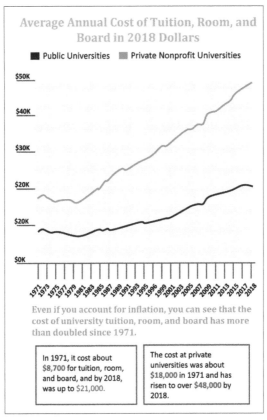

Average Annual Cost of Tuition, Room, and Board in 2018 Dollars

■ Public Universities   ■ Private Nonprofit Universities

Even if you account for inflation, you can see that the cost of university tuition, room, and board has more than doubled since 1971.

In 1971, it cost about $8,700 for tuition, room, and board, and by 2018, was up to $21,000.

The cost at private universities was about $18,000 in 1971 and has risen to over $48,000 by 2018.

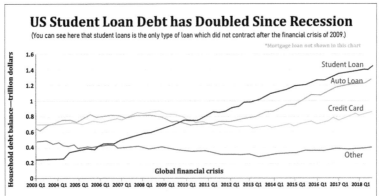

US Student Loan Debt has Doubled Since Recession

(You can see here that student loans is the only type of loan which did not contract after the financial crisis of 2009.)

*Mortgage loan not shown in this chart

The student loan situation in America broken down.[3]

73

much they are as a long-term inconvenience. But striking a proper balance and still being able to save even a small amount of money along with making your student loan payments should not be an afterthought.

Taking a Breath: How Do You Feel?

Well, team, are you ready to keep digging in? I hope that Instagram or Twitter hasn't come calling for you to check that most recent post or picture, because we're just getting started. (Don't worry; Ben and Anna are still going to be taking beach shots tomorrow!) These first few chapters deal primarily with basic money-management principles that are universal in nature: they all suggest ways to start thinking differently about money, income, and financial success.

I genuinely believe that if you take nothing else from this book but a hyper-aware focus on saving more money and the need for a consistent process that allows you to do so, your financial plan will be drastically improved. Just like if you are trying to get in better shape and do nothing but change your daily breakfast from a bacon, egg, and cheese bagel (what you want) to an egg-white omelet with spinach and a fruit salad (what you need), you'll find yourself, as if by magic, getting healthier. As we'll explore further, it takes a lot more than this to achieve the sort of success we're striving for, but it's not such a bad starting point.

5

Do You Have a
Written Financial Plan?

*"The economy depends about as
much on economists as the weather
does on weather forecasters."*
–Jean-Paul Kauffmann

Our firm is fortunate that so many of our clients feel comfortable introducing us to their family and friends. In fact, this is the most common way that we meet new people. We truly love being given the opportunity to take care of the most important people in our clients' lives, as we believe it's an incredible sign of trust in our team and our approach. But regardless of whether we are introduced to our client's best friend of thirty years or we're approached by a stranger who visited our website, our process begins the same way. Before we discuss any sort of investments vehicles or funds, or propose any actionable recommendations, we have to explore every relevant piece of a client's financial world.

Think about it like this: when you go to your doctor because you're feeling under the weather, he or she doesn't immediately prescribe you medicine for strep throat, right? Typically, Dr. Jones will check your height and weight; analyze your breathing, your throat, your nose, and your ears; check to see if you have a fever; and ask you how long you've been feeling sick, what you've done over the last three days, what you've eaten, and so on and so forth. The doctor will continue to poke and pry, asking all sorts of questions and running various checks that I'm definitely not qualified to discuss, having not taken a science class since my sophomore year of high school. Regardless, the doctor is going to have to know every single thing about your body, your family, your personal history, and your current physical makeup before moving forward. In other words, he or she is going to do a full medical checkup.

Your Financial Life Plan: A 360-Degree View

Well, our role, fundamentally, is the same as it pertains to your financial world. In fact, when we meet someone new, we both have to commit to completing this financial checkup, which we call our Financial Life Plan (FLIP™), before taking on any further tasks.

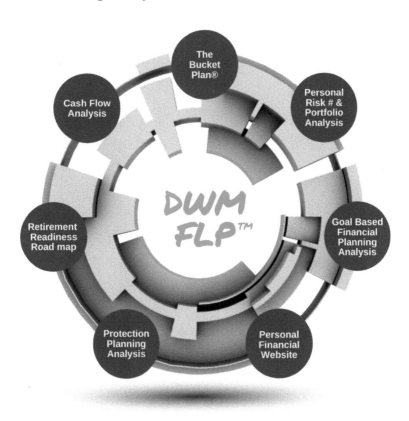

This FLIP will take into account all of the following factors:

- Goals
- Cash flow
- Assets and liabilities
- Budget and expense tracking
- Protection planning
- Investment risk tolerance
- Asset allocation
- Retirement planning
- Tax planning
- Estate planning
- Existing investments

The very first action step our clients take in creating their FLIP is walking us through everything they've done financially that has brought them to this point in time. We set them up with their own planning "portal" and go step by step in pulling everything together. That means, with our team holding their hand, they need to add their bank accounts, investments, retirement accounts, credit cards, and outstanding loans (such as a mortgage) onto their new planning page. We'll need to know how all their assets and liabilities are titled (are they owned individually, jointly, through a trust, are there transfer on death designations, etc.). Then, together, we'll add their salaries, bonuses, and other sources of income if there are any, as well as any stock options or equity they may be offered. They'll also add all of their existing insurance plans (term or permanent life insurance, disability insurance, long-term-care insurance, etc.) and the cost for each.

Next, they'll have to account for all of their fixed and variable monthly living expenses. As you might imagine, this can be a particularly eye opening part of the process (especially you've never really tracked how much and to where you're spending your money.) Along with the initial invitation to the planning portal, we send all new FLIP clients an empty budget form for them to fill out piece by piece. Sometimes clients already maintain their own Excel doc with a budget breakdown and so they don't need ours, cool! And a lot of time, clients don't have a "budget" per se but know that their monthly spending tops out at $5,000, and that gets the job done as well! Our focus, at this point, is not on remedying your spending habits but just acknowledging what they are so we can eventually project your cash flow into the future.

We'll need to get a better understanding of their current estate planning reality (particularly if it's a married couple or young family). Part of our responsibility in delivering the plan is to delve into the financial consequences of a premature passing and what estate planning risks the family is most vulnerable to (and how to rectify each issue). Are there guardianships for the kids currently in place if both parents passed away? Do they each have living wills, health care proxies, and a durable power of attorney? For the moment, all we need is a simple yes/no to these sorts of questions as we're just looking to gain a clearer picture of how things currently stand. The advice, recommendations, and solutions come later.

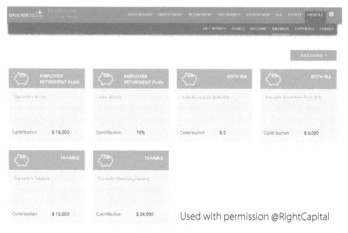

Used with permission @RightCapital

A snapshot of a sample client's savings.

As seen above, the clients will input how much they're saving each year into their various bank and investment accounts. Because we want this to be an accurate representation of where our clients stand today, we want the amount that they say they're saving to reflect what they're *currently* saving, not what they *could* be saving. We'll further add their student loan payments as well as any mortgages and rent payments they're responsible for (these are treated separately from your monthly discretionary spending) and specify when these responsibilities will end. Simply put, we need to know everything a client has done to this point in his or her financial life; this becomes the baseline to everything that might come after!

The last input the client will add at the start of the planning process, and the most important, are his or her financial goals. In some ways, this is the first step in creating "the plan," as everything that has come before it is about taking inventory and getting us all up to speed. This is not to make light of the "gathering" stage. You would be shocked to hear how many times new clients, after going through this process with us, realize that they still have an old 401(k), insurance policy, or brokerage account that they forgot even existed! That's why we go through this step relentlessly. Together, we'll comb through it all!

Can You Articulate Your Financial Goals?

Now, onto your goals! Any comprehensive financial plan worthy of its name has to start and end with your goals. One of the greatest ways we provide value to our clients is by framing the conversation about money in a different way than they've ever really thought about it: by making them write down their financial goals and basing everything else we discuss around those tangible targets. This part may sound intuitive and even obvious to you as you think, "Heck, I think about my financial goals every week, I want to have had a beach house yesterday!" That's great (really!), but have you put pen to paper and estimated all the details—what year you actually want to make that beach house happen, how much it'll cost, how it'll affect your current mortgage, how much time you're planning on spending there and how that might affect your business, travel costs, etc.? Thinking about your financial goals in this defined, quantifiable, and step-by-step way is the change we want to inspire as we move through the financial planning process.

As you move through the planning portal, you will begin to enter in these lifetime financial goals. These goals can be as vague, locked in, realistic, or optimistic as you want; nothing is written in stone at this point in your life, so we're really just creating targets to aim for. These specified goals can be for any and every time period in your life: one to three years out, five to seven years in the future, and those ten years and more. This is just a starting point, but you do actually have to input your answers. What are you trying to achieve? Why are you building wealth? What are you passionate about doing? On a more immediate level, is putting the kids through college Priority A? Is being able to take three months off to backpack through Asia number one on the list in the next five years? Is moving from a two-income household to a one-income household feasible? Naturally, we will walk you through the goal defining process but it absolutely requires some thought, attention, and time on your end as well…after all, it's your life we're planning for!

Jessica and her husband Brian, a young couple both twenty-nine years old, with whom I met recently wanted their goals to reflect a seven-year period, starting when they were each thirty-three, in which Jessica would stop working and take care of their kids (who didn't exist yet). They wanted to see what living on a one-income salary over that time period would look like and how much stress it could put on their ability to fund all of their other goals. As my team got to work building out their plan, we understood that making this lifestyle change feasible was a top priority for Jessica and Brian. Our recommendations would need to show what they had to change now in order to get there (or how far away this particular goal landed them from achieving their other goals).

The Wine Bar of Our Dreams

Another couple had a more unique goal. The husband, John, a fireman and his wife Janice, a business executive, wanted to fulfill a dream of theirs and buy a wine bar near their home. It was something they had always dreamed about but never actually thought they'd be able to do. As we went through one of our planning calls, Janice finally brought it up, almost hesitantly, as if even announcing it out loud was too stressful. When she finally did, I immediately burst out, "That's amazing!" Now, at this stage of the process, I had no idea if this wine bar was doable in the next five years or even how truly committed they were to the idea, but I loved that they were putting it all out on the table and vocalizing their dreams into actionable goals! We immediately got to work and built it into their plan in order to show them how feasible it was and what they would have to do to make it happen. The conversation is ongoing but they each have a much better idea of where they stand in relation to the epic wine bar of their dreams!

Knowing everything about your goals and future dreams is not just for me and my team but for you too. Because only once you realize what your goals and dreams are, can we do our best to help you get there or give you realistic expectations for what's attainable (or not) moving forward. But we have to be actually aiming toward something before we can determine in which direction to move.

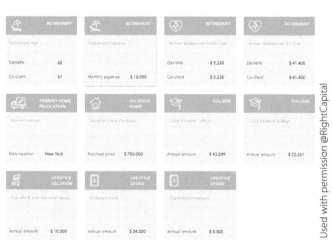

A snapshot of a sample client's future goals.

Here are some common goals that I typically run through with my H.E.N.R.Y. clients:

- Buying an engagement ring
- Wedding fund
- Buying a first home
- Future/current children's education goals (private school, religious school, university, etc.)
- Annual vacation budget
- Buying a second home for the growing family
- Childcare
- Moving from a two-household income to a one-household income
- Changing careers to more/less annual income
- Grad school
- Early retirement
- Retiring but performing consulting work
- Moving across the country to a more/less expensive area

To be honest, I can keep going, as there are so many goals out there, and it would be impossible to list everything I've heard over the last few years, but I think you get the idea. All of these goals come with costs, occur at different time periods and for varied amounts of time, and will result in changing financial obligations for an individual or a young family.

Renting versus Buying

Let's spend a brief moment on one goal in particular, because the subject comes up in almost every single one of my workshops; it's obviously on most of our minds! That is: to rent or buy a home. How do you know when it makes sense to buy a home and how can you gauge just how much you can truly afford to spend on a place once you're committed to buying? Let's dive in.

First off, I think most of us understand that owning your own home is "better" than renting it. You're building up your own equity in an asset that will one day be yours to sell, rent out for income, pass on to family, etc. It's *your* property and you will, in some way, reap the benefits of owning your own home later on down the road. Renting, on the other hand, is nothing more than an expense. Your monthly rent check provides a roof over your head for a given period of time, but once you move out, you have nothing to show for all of the money you've paid out over the years.

That said, buying a home is a difficult process—one that takes time and may not even be something you're ready to do just yet. Maybe you're getting moved around for work or maybe you just want the flexibility to move around in the coming years for any opportunity that presents itself (career, relationship, family). In this case, renting might be the answer that makes the most sense for you. More importantly, and as it relates to our role as financial planners, saving up enough money to put a down payment on a home and then pay a monthly mortgage (which is usually more than rent once you consider other costs, like HOA, property taxes, etc.)

are both large financial undertakings. At DWM, we want all our clients to have a better understanding of how buying a home would affect the rest of their planning goals. A lot of people don't. I see it all too often…so many young people get SO excited to buy their first home (understandably so) that they tend to overestimate their ability to pay a high mortgage, and they don't often think through the ramifications of a large down payment.

Salary Needed to Buy a House in Major US Cities

You may have the salary to afford a home, but it's not just the mortgage payment that you should think about.[4]

Yes, you might be able to technically to afford that dream home, but over time it can curtail your ability to advance any of your other financial priorities, leaving you "house poor" (an unfortunate descriptor for people that spend too high a percentage of their total income towards their mortgage, property taxes, utilities, etc.). And, over time, that mortgage may start to stress you out and feel like an unnecessary and overwhelming burden that can emotionally take its toll on you and potentially anybody else you're living with. As you can imagine, one of the Financial Life Plan's™ most important functions for new clients contemplating whether to buy (and how much to spend) is to illustrate how this housing goal dovetails with their other financial priorities.

Once our new clients have finished onboarding to their portal, we'll have a meeting to discuss the goals they've included and the first step is to have a conversation about everything they've indicated, just to make sure that we're all on the same page. Oftentimes, talking with a new client about their articulated goals after they've had some time to think about them, allows for a more accurate picture to come into focus. For example, we are usually able to ask if it's realistic that they would still be spending that same $3,000 per month in five years when they may have a spouse and kids. Or we'll account for the fact that buying a home in New York costs more than doing so in Philadelphia and this might prompt them to really consider whether or not they plan to live in New York long term. We may even talk through the idea that some parents are committed to an expensive private school while others believe in public education. And we'll note that some couples need to spend less on childcare because of the availability of family help, etc. All of these conversations help our clients to visualize the "reality" of their lives in the next year, five years, ten years, and so on.

We will include as many goals as the client mentions, and, in fact, we always recommend that they identify and include any goal that they're even remotely considering because we want this plan to be as comprehensive as possible. We can always remove the goals (and their accompanying cost) later, but the more goals that clients add at the start, the more helpful the analysis of their financial picture will be for us. Put another way, we want to plan for as many future costs as we can. If the plan works, meaning you're on track to hit all of your goals, and five years later, it turns out that your daughter earned a scholarship and you don't need to pay for college anymore, awesome! You're in even better shape than we thought! But as the plan is all about how to get prepared for what's to come, we would rather overshoot the runway rather than leave anything up to chance.

The Planning Process Is Just the Beginning

Once we have all of the necessary information, the planning process becomes an ongoing dialogue between our team and the client to ensure that we're moving in the right direction. One of the very first things I tell a client when we begin this process is that the plan is written, metaphorically, in pencil. We can make changes to it at any time, and, in fact, we almost certainly will be making changes in the years to come. The FLIP that starts every new client relationship is simply the beginning of the road map, a snapshot of your current situation, something that will allow the haziness of the future to begin to dissipate.

To be clear, the client will pay us a fee for this written plan and analysis. We charge clients for the time, work, and expertise we put into the plan before we even discuss managing their investable assets because they must have skin in the game and be committed to the process. We also want the plan to stand alone as an objective plan free from any conflict of interest that would come if the plan was only meant to persuade you to have our team manage your investments afterward. No, the FLIP stands alone as a complete, all-encompassing roadmap, even if we don't end up working together (more on that below, because it's super important!).

> We want clients who are as committed and invested in their family's future as we are, and if they haven't paid for the plan, how committed will they be to listen to our analysis or heed the plan's recommendations?

Simply put, we want clients who are as committed and invested in their family's future as we are, and if they haven't paid for the plan, how committed will they be to listen to our analysis or heed the plan's recommendations? To be sure, there are "financial plans" out there that you can complete for free, but is there anything of genuine value that you've received for free in any area of your life? We want clients who understand, at the outset of our relationship, how crucial the comprehensive planning process is to everything that might follow. Without this, any work that we might do together in the future is built on a shaky foundation that will crumble at some point down the road. No thank you!

As you read the previous paragraphs about what our financial plan entails, you may have been checking off everything in your head and patting yourself on the back. Budget? Yup! Debt-management strategy? Already on it. Insurance planning? Done! If that's the case, awesome! Going through the planning-software input process with clients who are clear about what they've already completed at this point in their life (and why) is a breeze. Even more importantly, when we reach the point of showing them their plan's probability of success, these people are typically in amazing shape. This group of people (the planners) are the most enthusiastic to sign up for our plan because they already understand how important planning is to their ultimate success! For them, our plan is basically an opportunity to get an expert second opinion to confirm that they're on the right path and that they didn't miss anything along the way.

The plan becomes a validation of their life choices. Cool. For them, our job is to fine-tune the plan along the edges and make their road ahead as smooth as possible.

Starting Is Half the Battle

It's also possible that while reading that list of planning areas, you slumped in your seat and hated me a bit more with each line. Trust me, I know, but that's why we're getting started. You know how they say showing up is half the battle? Well, so is lifting the curtain and making a commitment to look at your financial world. I have seen so many clients over the years admit that they failed to plan, or delayed their planning for years, simply because they didn't really *want* to know where they stood or how far behind they were. The possibility of having to confront their own spending habits, investment choices, and financial behaviors was not something they wanted to explore. For them, ignorance had been bliss.

Every time I hear that sentiment, it brings me back to my time as a paratrooper in the IDF. Throughout our training, we would have periodic long and brutal marches through the night with all of our gear and weapons weighing us down. Our first march was four kilometers, and our final march, to complete our training, was seventy kilometers through the mountains leading to Jerusalem. We completed approximately a dozen marches of increasing distance throughout our seven months of training.

An amazing thing happened during this process. More people dropped out of our unit during the four- and eight-kilometer marches at the start than did during the much

Taken at the end of the most difficult week of training which culminated in a 65km march through the mountains of Jerusalem. Here I am with my dad who greeted me at the end!

more agonizing thirty- and forty-kilometer marches that followed. Now, to set the stage, everyone in my unit had to try out to become a paratrooper, so these guys were in great shape. Everyone was capable of marching four kilometers in his sleep (and with how little we actually slept, this isn't hyperbole!). But, looking back, after all of the craziness that the army threw our way, I realize that these individuals had quit during the four-kilometer march not because that particular march was so difficult, but because in their head, as they were walking four kilometers, they were imagining themselves attempting the fifty-kilometer march, and the idea destroyed them. They couldn't come to grips with the fact that they would have to endure that when the time came. Their thinking was, *If I'm hurting now, that longer one is going to be impossible, so I think it's better to bow out now.*

I've seen that same level of paralysis take hold of otherwise successful young professionals. It can be easier to just keep grinding along in your career and continue making

> It can be easier to just keep grinding along in your career and continue making more money, and hope that your financial future will simply work itself out. Maybe it will; that's a possibility. But do you want to take that chance?

more money, and hope that your financial future will simply work itself out. Maybe it will; that's a possibility. But do you want to take that chance?

OK, rant over. Let's talk about the plan.

What Will Your FLIP Plan Show?

What happens once we have all the information that we need to get started? The most fun part for you: our team gets to work! Internally, we begin to analyze your current financial situation and determine if you're on track toward achieving your goals. Are your investments in line with your goals and predetermined risk tolerance? Are you saving enough money each month to pay for both graduate school and a first home? Is there enough insurance to pay off the mortgage in the case of a disaster? Are your spending habits leaving you with a worrisome amount in your retirement accounts after accounting for vacation-home costs? At the current rate, will you be working until you're eighty years old?

The plan may actually reveal itself to be three plans: showing you retiring at fifty-five, sixty, and sixty-five, each with different assumptions and lifestyles built in, and identifying your probability of success in hitting your goals in each scenario. They may further show you buying your first home at thirty, thirty-four, and thirty-seven so that you can see all of the possibilities. None of these projections are meant to be definitive in any way, but, rather, are meant to give you a snapshot of where you stand today and further clarity on the direction you're headed if you don't change your course. They may also include recommendations to make changes if need be.

Let's look back at the example I mentioned earlier regarding Dan and Linda (the lifestyle-creep story) to show what will happen to your net worth ten years out if you were to increase your monthly savings from $1,000 to $2,000, and how this will move the needle on your plan's ultimate probability of success.

When we get to the point of delivering all of this information to you as part of the plan's cash flow analysis, the objective is not to give you perfect clarity (because we can't), but, rather, to start laying the concrete foundation and give you context for the choices to come.

The last part of the financial planning process is when we make our plan recommendations: changes you can make in your financial life to help bring you closer to the ultimate achievement of your goals. These recommendations may take the form of new or modified investment strategies, wealth creation account planning, estate planning and family protection measures, debt management plans, lifestyle downsizing, or education funding, to name a few. Some may be as simple (and yet crucial) as making sure your assets are titled properly and that you understand what it means for accounts to be joint, transfer on death (TOD), individual, etc. We'll show you how our recommendations will increase your plan's probability of success, why we're making these recommendations, the order of priority for implementing everything we're discussing, and exactly how we would implement these recommendations changes should we continue working together.

The last part of that sentence, "should we continue working together," is crucial.

Unbiased and Objective Advice Is the Key

One of the most important parts of this whole process is the mutual understanding that the client is under no obligation to make our recommended changes with us—or even make those changes at all. When we get to that part of the process, the FLIP Delivery Meeting, the client is totally free to take his or her plan and hit the road! We separate the financial check-up, analysis, and recommendations (which together make up the FLIP) from the actual implementation steps because we think it's important that our clients know that they are 100 percent free to implement our recommendations with anyone they choose. The merits of the plan are in no way contingent upon working with us going forward. Of course, we hope that our clients will continue to work with us for decades to come, and that's what happens about 90 percent of the time, but affording our clients that choice after the check-up is important to both us and them! The plan doesn't come with any caveats or expectations; we want to give objective, unbiased advice that you're paying us to give.

If I haven't made the creation of the financial plan seem crucial enough, allow me to drill a bit further to drive the point home. We have had prospects come to us with $1 million to $5 million, who are primarily concerned with having us manage their investments. They've been led to believe that "investment management" is financial planning, and so they don't want the plan. Those clients have been respectfully turned away. While losing those potential clients is frustrating for us, we're committed to our process. In addition, we know that without any sort of plan driving the investment strategy, it's only a matter of time before that client strays the course. How could we really build a portfolio attuned to a client's goals, lifestyle, cash flow, and income needs if we haven't done all that planning first? It's putting the cart before the horse.

I know what you're thinking: there are millions of financially successful American families that have not completed a Drucker Wealth Financial Life Plan. It's shocking...but true. You may have your own advisor. You may manage your finances on your own. You may live on the other side of the world. Cool! My aim in walking you through what *our* process to get started looks like is not to explain our specifics, but, rather, our focus. However you choose to start (or restart) thinking about your financial life, your goals, and a comprehensive plan should be the starting point. The investment strategies, vehicles, portfolios, and products should only come later.

6

The Power of Equities Over Time

"Investing should be more like watching paint dry or watching grass grow. If you want excitement take $800 and go to Las Vegas."
–Paul Sameulson

For many pages now, I've been discussing the importance of saving money, living below your means, and having a goal-driven plan. But let's say you've done all that. Where exactly should you be putting all that money that you're now so motivated and excited to be saving? In other words, what happens next? Of course, a definitive answer to that question requires a real understanding of your financial needs, identification of your time horizon, and a one-on-one conversation, but there are timeless principles that can help form the foundation of the answer.

These principles will form the crux of the next few chapters. I mentioned, at the outset of the book, that there were certain financial advisors/authors when I was just starting out that influenced my path as an advisor. My dad would send me their speeches, articles, and books while I was at university and in the military. One author stands alone. I would be remiss if I didn't publicly thank and show my appreciation to a financial advisor, author, and public speaker that my dad and I both call our "financial guru." Mr. Nick Murray. I have read his books dozens of times over the years, circling back periodically for extra inspiration and emphasis as needed, and I urge every single of one of you to start by reading his book *Simple Wealth, Inevitable Wealth* (his book, as well as a few others, are listed in the back of my book in the recommended reading section). I didn't quote, paraphrase, or directly reference any of Mr. Murray's book below unless where specified, but as I have internalized so much of his wit and wisdom over the years, I would find it hard to believe that his messages didn't shine through at various points throughout my explanations. Again, to Mr. Murray, (who will receive one of the book's very first copies), if you're reading this…thank you…other than my own flesh and blood, you have been the most important "professor" I've ever had.

Some Financial Terms Briefly Defined

Before getting into the investment principles themselves, let's define a few terms that are going to be compared and broken down over the next few subjects: stocks/equities, bonds/fixed income, diversification, and risk. If you're well versed in these areas, feel free to skip ahead a bit or just skim through this section while daydreaming about what you'll eat for dinner tonight. I can only hope you're being cautious with your spending money after having read the first few chapters of this book!

You would be surprised by how many smart, successful, and well-rounded young professionals aren't totally clear on the difference between a stock and a bond and feel it's too late to ask someone to explain it. Not to go all "We live in a society in which…" on you, but this actually traces back to an issue with the current American education system. It is truly astounding that to graduate high school, we needed to know what a sine curve is, but we never learned how to balance a checkbook, how to budget a paycheck, how a mortgage works, or the difference between basic investable assets like stocks, bonds, or certificates of deposit. My intuition tells me that at least one of those personal-finance concepts may have arisen in your life over the past five years, but a sine curve has made nary an appearance since eleventh-grade algebra! As a result, it's common for these financial concepts to be thrust upon a young professional for the first time right as they're starting their own careers (and learning everything they need to for their day-to-day job) without much time or energy to focus on them. Let's rectify that.

Let's keep it simple. Owning a stock means that you have an actual ownership stake in that business, while owning a bond means, effectively, that you're loaning money to the company, with the assumption that you will be paid back in a certain number of years with interest paid along the way. Let's use a real company as an example. If you were to buy one share of Apple stock, that means that you now own a (very small) stake in Apple. As Apple's value (and by that, we mean the company's

> Owning a stock means that you have an actual ownership stake in that business, while owning a bond means, effectively, that you're loaning money to the company, with the assumption that you will be paid back in a certain number of years with interest paid along the way.

assets and earnings) increases or decreases, your one share of stock will be worth more or less proportionally to your ownership interest. So if Apple continues to rise in value, the sky's the limit for the value of your shares in Apple company stock. You will keep making money as long as Apple grows in value because you actually own a small piece of the company. There is nothing limiting your earning potential. Likewise, if Apple were to lose 80 percent of its value, your ownership stake (your one share of stock) would also be worth 80 percent less, and if the company went out of business, your stock would become worthless! Stocks are referred to as "equities," which makes sense, as we just described stocks as owning "equity" in a company.

Owning a bond works differently. When you buy a ten-year bond in Apple, for example, you're loaning that money (at whatever the price of that bond) to Apple and Apple is agreeing to pay the money back to you in ten years' time (as long as they're financially able to.) Each year along the way, you will be paid interest as an income stream, dependent upon the interest rate established by the company at the time of your bond's issue. This is called a bond's yield. To use the previous example, if you owned an Apple bond that cost you $10 to buy, it wouldn't matter if Apple's value had tripled when you're looking to redeem (get your money back) from the bond. You will still be owed $10. You're not a part of that company's growth because you don't own a piece of the company; you just lent the company money at a certain interest rate.

Again, think about it on a much smaller and more personal scale: if you loaned your friend money for his startup venture, your degree of risk and reward is a lot less than his, who, as an owner, has it all on the line. It's for this reason that bonds are oftentimes referred to as "fixed income," because you know what that income should be each year and there's generally less fluctuation to the price of your bond than if you owned stock in that company instead. Of course, there is nevertheless some fluctuation to the price of the bond over time.

To simplify our understanding of one of the main risks to the price of your bonds over time, I'll just say this: the value of your bonds will largely work inversely with current interest rates. So, if interest rates are going up that means the value of the bonds you currently own will go down. The simplest explanation for why this is true is that if interest rates are rising, you would be able to buy newer bonds with a higher yield (aka more income due) so the bonds you own already would be less valuable. Again, none of this is particularly important for our conversation, but I wanted to complete our breakdown of stocks & bonds so that we're ready to move on to the good stuff.

For the rest of this book, when I discuss equities, I'm referring to the asset class as a whole and not any one company's stock, because my point is never to highlight any particular company or recommend any specific stock. This is a matter of course; we're not in the prognosticating business, and recommending any one stock, or having so much of your money tied up in any one's company's fate, actually feels an awful lot like gambling. Any company can disappear (like Enron, Blockbuster, Toys "R" Us, Lehman Brothers Holdings Inc., etc.) and less drastically, any one company vastly under or performance expectations. The variance for any one company is through the roof! In fact, let's play a game: If I were to say right now that you could go back to 2004 and invest in one of two companies that are about to become public, Google and Dominos, which would you have chosen?

Source: Charlie Bello, Compound Capital Advisors. Chart courtesy of StockCharts.com.

Now, this is not to be beat up on Google (which as you can see has done phenomenally and, c'mon, is one of the greatest companies in the world) but rather to show the vagaries of "betting" on any one company!

Instead, when I discuss the power of owning equities and their remarkable ability to compound wealth over time (as I'm about to), I'm referring to owning the asset class as a whole, because, practically speaking, the entire asset class can't go to zero. For the stock market as an entire asset class to no longer be rewarding to investors, companies of varying sizes, sectors, and geographic locales would have to lose money consistently, repeatedly, and relentlessly for a significant period of time. If this were to happen, trust me, your stock portfolios will be the least of your worries: we should all head for the hills and load up on ammo and canned goods because the economic apocalypse would be upon us. As I'm sure you're aware, this sort of economic meltdown without a corresponding recovery has never happened in the entire history of the stock market. By the way, referring to stocks as the entire asset class as a way to spread around our risk (and ultimately to lower it) is the textbook definition of diversification. To our mind, the concept is even simpler: not owning enough of any one company to make a killing from its rise or to get killed by its fall.

The Stock Market Over Time

Welcome back to everyone who skipped ahead. My dad has a saying (I'm 99 percent sure he took it from someone else, but I've heard it from him for so long that I'll reluctantly give him credit): "It's not about timing the market; it's time *in* *the* market." For us young people, no part of our investment strategy will be more important than the amount of time we allow ourselves to be a part of the growing American and world economy.

"Wait!" you say. "How do I know the market is growing? Aren't we poised for a big market correction after eight years of upward momentum?" Of course we are—although I have no idea if it's going to be in six weeks, six months, or six years. However, for us young folks, that hardly matters because these short-term movements are irrelevant to the sort of long-term growth I'm describing.

DATES OF MARKET PEAK	DATES OF MARKET TROUGH	% RETURN	DURATION	MARKET PEAK	MARKET TROUGH
05/29/46	06/13/49	-29.5%	36.5 mos.	19.3	13.6
08/02/56	10/22/57	-21.5%	14.5 mos.	49.7	39.0
12/12/61	06/26/62	-28.0%	6.5 mos.	72.6	52.3
02/09/66	10/07/66	-22.2%	8.0 mos.	94.1	73.2
11/29/68	05/26/70	-36.0%	18.0 mos.	108.4	69.3
01/11/73	10/03/74	-48.0%	20.5 mos.	120.2	62.3
09/21/76	03/06/78	-19.4%	17.5 mos.	107.8	86.9
11/28/80	08/12/82	-27.0%	20.5 mos.	140.5	102.4
08/25/87	12/04/87	-33.5%	3.5 mos.	336.8	223.9
07/16/90	10/11/90	-20.0%	3.0 mos.	369.0	295.5
07/17/98	08/31/98	-19.3%	1.5 mos.	1186.8	957.3
03/24/00	10/09/02	-49.2%	30.5 mos.	1527.5	776.7
10/09/07	03/09/09	-57.0%	17.0 mos.	1565.1	676.5
04/29/11	10/3/11	-19.4%	5.0 mos.	1363.6	1099.2
09/20/18	12/24/18	-19.8%	3.0 mos.	2930.8	2351.1

© Nick Murray, July 2017.

Check out the chart above from Nick Murray. Whether we like to admit it or not, stock prices go down all the time! Between 1946 and 2016, according to Nick, "there were 14 bear markets in stocks, usually defined as a decline in the (S&P 500) Index of 20% or more on a closing basis." That means that we'll see a 20 percent drop in the stock market, on average, once every five years! Even more astonishing, over those same seventy years, there have been fifty-seven market corrections of at least 10 percent; that's about once every fifteen months! Again, once every fifteen months, on average, the S&P 500 stock index will lose 10 percent of its value! (Reread those last two sentences until you truly understand how frequently we're talking here.)[5]

What's crucial to keep in mind is that these stock prices don't stay down for long. Despite these frequent dips, the stock market as a whole (using the broad index representing the American stock market, the S&P 500 that we just referenced as a bogie) has increased 150 times over during that same time period. Put another way, the S&P 500 Index price was fifteen back in 1946. It had climbed to 600 when my dad was born in 1963 and it was at 1,900 in 1991, when I was born. It's currently around 30,000.[6]

On the following page is a graph of what that consistent upward movement looks like over time.

By any possible measure, the past eighty years have shown consistent upward movement. I love this particular graph of the stock market over time, because it names every 'crisis of the moment' throughout history and we get to see how every single one of them, no matter how scary at the time, was ultimately irrelevant to the stock market's continued advancement. And, as we just saw, every single dip in the market is followed by a significant and permanent

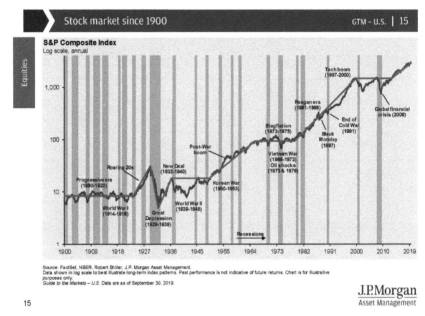

Source: J.P. Morgan Asset Management and Guide to the Markets [Q4, September 2019]

upward climb that we all get to be a part of. Those declines have not once, not ever, managed to stop the unrelenting upward trajectory of the stock market, which, as you can see for yourself in the next chart, has meant an average annual return in excess of 10 percent. Meanwhile, over that same period of time, bonds have resulted in a rate of return between 5 and 6 percent.

After accounting for inflation (the loss of our money's purchasing power over time) at 2.9 percent annually, that means that bonds historically have provided us with about half (!) the stock market's real rate of return over the past seventy years!

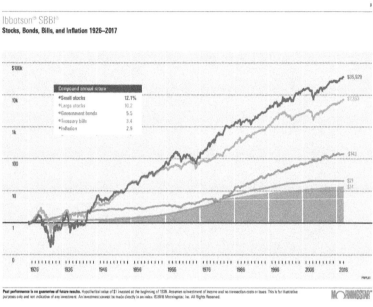

Ibbotson® SBBI®
Stocks, Bonds, Bills, and Inflation 1926–2017

Short-Term Volatility versus Long-Term Risk

OK, I have to pause for a moment so that you can reread that last paragraph again, while asking yourselves why exactly, stocks are considered a "risky" investment and bonds less so? Didn't we just determine that historically stocks grossly outperform bonds?!

It's time to shine a magnifying light on the words "risk" and "volatility," and how we constantly conflate the two to our own detriment. Let's start with volatility. Volatility, strictly speaking, means the amount of movement or gyration away from the investment's mean/average over any period of time. In other words, does the investment's price bounce around a lot? That's all it means. An asset that's "volatile" will fluctuate frequently between highs and lows, but an investment's volatility actually says nothing about the broader direction that your investment is moving over a period of time i.e.: is your money going up or down over time.

The stock market is exceedingly volatile. Money invested in the stock market will wildly fluctuate in value over any short amount of time. In fact, from 1980 through 2016, for example, the stock market had an average inter-year swing of 14 percent annually. Take a look:

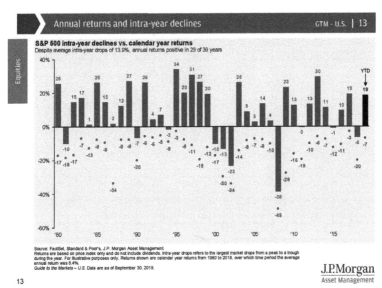

Source: J.P. Morgan Asset Management and Guide to the Markets [Q4, 2013]

This means that the difference between the stock market's high and low within each calendar year was quite dramatic, spanning 14 percentage points on average. That's a lot of movement. Stuff goes up and down a lot even within every calendar year! OK, so we know now, investing in the stock market is volatile.

As Daniel Crosby, New York Times Best Selling Author of *The Behavioral Investor*, has said, "Bumpy markets aren't necessarily bad markets." In fact, this volatility works to our favor over the long term as that same chart makes clear: twenty-nine of the thirty-nine years shown ended up! Short-term volatility is the price we pay for the higher returns that we will accrue over time by owning stocks. Capitalism rewards those that supply capital to the system and are accountable for it. That's why, as we already discussed, it's better to be an owner of capital (think about why you inherently want to own rather than rent your home) than a borrower of capital.

Not only does this make sense, but it also actually has to be true that in exchange for the stress and uncertainty inherent to the short-term volatility of stocks (omg, did you see the news…the stock market went down 20 percent today!), we get the reward of consistent long-term gains. If stocks didn't, over time, outperform more conservative asset classes, there would be no reason for us to endure their short-term swings! Why drive ourselves crazy for no upside? If all asset classes performed about the same over the long term, we would naturally elect to invest in vehicles that don't freak out as much day-to-day (meaning they're less volatile). But that's not the case.

As you can see in the next chart, going back all the way to 1926(!), stocks have consistently provided substantially better returns than conservative asset classes like bonds or cash, and *every single* fifteen-year rolling period through this same eighty-plus-year period has had positive returns, even with all that craziness/volatility along the way. In other words, historically speaking, investing for a period of time longer than fifteen years, historically, has removed the risk of losing money in the stock market! Can you see why this might be an extremely powerful thing for us young people to internalize as soon as possible? As long as we know we're in it for the long term—and as we will soon discuss we most certainly are—we shouldn't sweat the temporary declines or the temporary volatility of the stock market.

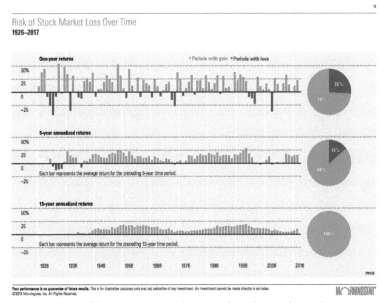

Every fifteen-year period invested in the stock market has resulted in positive returns!

OK, so the stock market goes up over time. I've shown you enough graphs and charts based on history stretching back almost one hundred years to convert you into an equity believer. You understand that equity investments losing money for a period of time longer than fifteen years would be unprecedented in the entire history of the stock market. I feel pretty good relying on that sort of legacy.

But let's ask a more philosophical question to explain the power of owning equities. Why does the stock market consistently go up over time? I'll answer by having you imagine that just yesterday, let's say, the stock market lost 20 percent in twenty-four hours (as we know this happens periodically and who knows, maybe it's happening as you're reading.) Are we really saying that overnight, some of the largest and most profitable companies in the world lost 20 percent of their value?

Do we really think that overnight, these companies are generating 20 percent less business and their employees are 20 percent less efficient than they were the previous day? Of course not! The stock market's temporary peaks and valleys represent mass hysteria and group think about what the future portends rather than being any reflection on the viability of the companies themselves. These companies are not fundamentally different than they were the previous day just because their price fluctuated. We, as investors, created the dramatic price change through our panicked reactions to the crisis of the moment (whatever that may be). Thinking about companies purely as stock prices makes investing seem almost like a game, and in games anything can happen. But when we're investing in the stock market, we're investing in actual companies and that's helpful to think about during market corrections.

In fact, from a historical perspective, that's the reason the stock market continuing to go up is the only rational thing that can possibly happen in the future. Without diverting too much into politics/philosophy, capitalism is inherently logical. Companies exist to be profitable and to make money for their owners and for their shareholders (yes there may be secondary goals, but that is directive number one).

If a company is not profitable for too long a period of time, it will be driven out of business by a better and more efficient business. As a result, the companies that make up the indexes reflecting the "stock market" are going to either keep profiting or be replaced by newer and better companies that will. Either way, the stock market as a whole should continue its upward climb. Simply put, investing in the stock market means investing your money in the world's ability to do business: companies are hardwired to continue growing profits over time.

Companies seeking the greatest profit, and adapting and changing and replacing one another as they need to in order to get there, is a feature, and not a temporary bug, of the entire system and it's what ensures the inevitable upward trend of the stock market, and on a larger level, the advancement of the world economy. Investing in their continued ability to do so is only rational and logical.

By the way, this whole section may seem like a very Wolf-of-Wall Street—"greed is good"—type of pronouncement but continued growth and improvement is not just a staple of companies seeking to profit: it's true of society at large. Human advancement and human achievement is the defining story of our collective history. Case in point: right now is the greatest time to be alive in human history. The world is better, more prosperous, safer, and healthier now than it was one hundred years ago and any time before that. By any possible metric (world poverty, illiteracy, infant mortality, world hunger) humanity is better off than we were in previous centuries; today's poor live better than the kings and queens of yesteryear. Take a look:

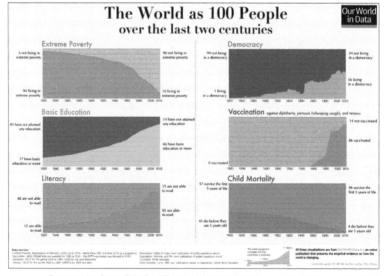

Source: Max Roser (2019) – "The World as 100 People over the last two centuries." Published online at OurWorldInData.org. Retrieved from: 'https://ourworldindata.org/uploads/2017/01/Two-centuries-World-as-100-people.png' [Online Resource]

Yes, the world can seem chaotic and cruel at times, and increasingly so (it may seem) in today's day and age, but I am eternally optimistic about the world we live in and humanity's abilities to solve the problems of tomorrow. One of Israel's founding fathers, David Ben Gurion, once said, "In Israel, to be a realist is to believe in miracles." Well, I don't know about miracles, but I'll say that being an optimist should be a pre-requisite for anyone that plans and invests their money for the future. To plan for the future means to believe in that future.

I apologize. When I get into a speech about the power of equities, I can black out and go on for days because it is just that important! So now that we have defined and described volatility, what does risk mean? I would define investment risk simply as the possibility that our investments will not allow us to achieve our goals. I would argue that the more "risk" a decision comes with, financial or otherwise, the higher the likelihood that the decision will lead us to failure (however we define failure for that particular decision). In this arena, failure means that our investments don't grow enough, and we don't have enough money to accomplish what we want to! How else can we define it? Well, if we just determined that over every single twenty-year period in history, stocks have outperformed bonds, which one is really the risky asset? Which asset gives us a higher probability of not having enough money over the long term? Bonds! Of course! As Nick Murray frequently proclaims in his books,

"The only real risk of stocks over the long term is not owning them!" (Murray, *Simple Wealth, Inevitable Wealth*)

When thinking about stocks, I believe the question to consider is this: Are we trying to limit the change in price fluctuations over the short term, or are we trying to ensure our money goes up more than it goes down over the long term? In other words, are we concerned about short-term volatility or the long-term risk of not having enough money to accomplish our goals? For us, as young investors specifically, why should we care about those temporary declines when we're investing for the next ten, fifteen, or twenty years?

Short-Term Saving versus Long-Term Investing

Now, let's be clear. I am absolutely *not* saying that you should be putting all of your money into the stock market! Of course not. First off, I wouldn't put all of my money in any one vehicle, asset class, or strategy. But more relevant to this conversation, being invested in the stock market only makes sense with money that *you don't need in the short term*. Let's dig deeper into this idea as I share a bit about my own planning.

I'm twenty-eight years old. I save money every month into my backdoor Roth IRA, SEP IRA, brokerage investment portfolios, and permanent insurance policy. The money I'm saving into these long-term vehicles is meant to remain invested for ten to fifteen-plus years. It's money that's intended to replace my income in retirement, pay my

future kids' college education, or buy a vacation home…
but it's not the money I need for my cash flow in the near
future. This is why I don't care about the next six months
of market volatility: I know that I have time to wait for any
potential short-term loss I suffer to rebound! Based on all
available history (which is the only thing we can go on),
those market declines are temporary but the gains I will
achieve by outlasting them are permanent. Here's what
those temporary declines and the following recoveries over
time have looked like when sketched out:

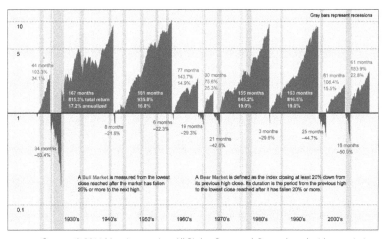

History of U.S. Bear & Bull Markets Since 1926,
and was sourced in an article by Bob Johnson titled,
"How Long Can the Bull Continue to Run."

As the visual makes obvious, the stock market recoveries
are longer, more powerful, and ultimately overwhelm any
of the losses that precipitated them and as a result the stock

market has kept climbing despite them. I look at that picture and think, "Cool, two steps back, ten steps forward…on repeat. Sign me up!" Here's the beautiful part: because we know, this decline is temporary, and we know further that the money we have invested is not intended for the near future, we're not going to freak out and make panicked decisions when doing so would mean missing out on all that long-term upside. For good measure, let's take one more look at that "long term upside."

S&P 500 Total Return Index and Historical Probabilities of a Profit

S&P 500 Annual Total Return	10.1%
Percentage up all 1-Day Periods	53.5%
Percentage up all 1-Month Periods	62.9%
Percentage up all 1-Year Periods	73.1%
Percentage up all 3-Year Periods	83.5%
Percentage up all 5-Year Periods	86.5%
Percentage up all 10-Year Periods	96.4%
Percentage up all 15-Year Periods	100.0%
Percentage up all 20-Year Periods	100.0%
Percentage up all 30-Year Periods	100.0%

Here's another way to think about it: markets fluctuate but do not create loss! *People* create loss by mistaking a temporary loss for permanent decline and trying to guess when to sell right before the market rebounds, as it always does. As long as we stay the course, understanding that we have a long-term focus with these particular assets, investing aggressively (owning stocks) will help us on our quest to achieve long-term financial success.

7

Our Emotions Want to Destroy Our Investments

"October: This is one of the particularly dangerous months to invest in stocks. Other dangerous months are July, January, September, April, November, May, March, June, December, August and February."
–Mark Twain

The Israel Defense Force is considered one of the top military forces in the world, and I am forever proud and humbled to have served in my Combat Paratrooper unit within the IDF. My time as a soldier was the greatest, most rewarding, and most memorable experi¬ence of my life. That said, as with every soldier since the Roman Centaurians, not every day was full of joy and fun.

One night we were moving from our guard post in the south of Israel to the border of Lebanon, up north. We got to the new base in the dead of night and immediately had to replace the unit that had been stationed there for the past few months. As luck would have it, I drew the first guard shift overlooking the border that night at around 3:00 a.m. After a short security briefing (in Hebrew and at a point in my service in which I was definitely *not* totally comfortable speaking the language), I went out to my post.

Enjoying a quick statuesque photo while on guard duty in Israel!

It was the middle of the night, so it was dark, quiet, and cold, and I couldn't see very far ahead of me. I really didn't know how close or far any potential threat was. The briefing had been rushed, and I'd understood *at best* every fourth word…really! So, at night, on a border, every sound feels like, well, like you're alone on a hostile military border. It's a little intense. I heard some crazy noises throughout the night, and I thought, *Holy shit, this is it. I, Gideon Drucker, am the first line of defense right now for the state of Israel. This cannot be good!!*

My heart was bursting, and I got on the walkie-talkie to speak with my friend Yarden, who was on an opposite post. We started talking, and I walked around my post trying to get a better sense of what was out there. There was nothing there. Eventually, I relaxed a bit, and I realized I hadn't heard anything for hours. I left my shift a few hours later, largely forgetting about the hour of panic that had consumed my entire being.

The next day, looking out from where I was the previous night, I had to laugh at myself. I saw that I had actually been standing a solid one hundred yards away from the real border of Lebanon, and that there was a wide-open field extending another quarter mile from the nearest Lebanese town. There was no way what I had heard all night was anything other than the fifty goats I had been looking at all night! I had been driving myself crazy over farm animals! If I had just been able to see out in the distance or had better information at the start, it would have been a walk-in-the-park, guard-duty shift, and any noises or weirdness along the way would have been totally manageable and normal—not anything to fret about. (Understand the parable?)

The Importance of Keeping Our Emotions in Check

Let's bring it back to our investing world. What are the murmurs and eerie shapes out in the darkness of the financial world? Our emotions! The way that we, as investors, react to investment performance can freak us out and overwhelm us to the point that we devastate any possible chance for investment success. We panic during market downturns, chase the hot fund in our portfolio when things are up, and develop irrational FOMO upon hearing that our neighbor is making more money in the market than we are. All of these moments that make us human and normal are also the most formidable challenge we face in achieving the sort of investment success we strive for. Here's what most of us look like emotionally as our investments ebb and flow over time.

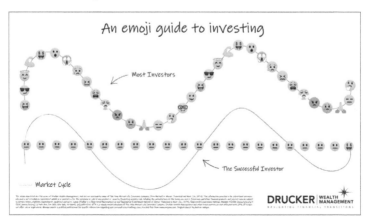

126

I bet you didn't think I would be using emoticons to explain one of the fundamental investing ideas of my book right? In fact, I use this every chance I get. As I mentioned, I'm asked to give workshops all over the New York area about avoiding H.E.N.R.Y. Syndrome and investing strategies for young people looking to get started, and this is always the most popular slide. Because so many people take pictures of the slide and story it for their Instagram pages, I actually wouldn't be surprised if you've already seen it somehow on social media, kind of like the whole Six Degrees of Kevin Bacon thing. Beyond just the ridiculousness of using emojis to describe the stock market, part of why it resonates so strongly with everyone is because it perfectly captures the way we react to our investments!

Think about the last time you saw your 401(k) statement after a particularly great quarter in the stock market. You were ecstatic. All of a sudden, making money in the market had become easy, and you thought about contributing even more to your 401(k) each month because it was climbing like crazy every single day you looked at it! You were upbeat and positively thrilled about your financial future. And then, as it always does, things took a turn, and the account started dropping. Hard. Eventually, it went down by 25 percent, and the $100,000 in your 401(k) that you had worked so hard to accumulate went down to $75,000 seemingly in the blink of an eye.

Now you were stressed. You began thinking about moving the rest of your account to cash because you couldn't stomach losing any more money. You were thinking that your advisor (if you had one) was an idiot, you didn't know why you even started investing in the first place, and why weren't you just hiding money under your bed like the good old days? This negativity went on for a while, until your account rebounded, as it always does. And this emotional rollercoaster continued month after month, quarter after quarter, as you reacted emotionally to the almost daily market fluctuations that we know, intellectually, are normal!

Our Emotions versus Our Performance

"OK," you say, "so what if we react too emotionally and that our moods, sleep patterns, and stress levels are too attached to whether my investments are up or down at the end of any given quarter? What does this have to do with the actual performance of my investments over time? It's not like my emotions are actually going to lead to worse results, right?" Au contraire. Without question, our emotions invariably lead us to making stupid, rash decisions out of fear and greed that end up causing us to underperform the very investments that we own! Take a look on the next page.

The point of this chart is not which of the asset classes has the highest return. The relevant takeaways are twofold. First, let's acknowledge that if you had owned any of these major asset classes held herein, or any combination of them, and then had done nothing with your investments, you would have averaged between 6 percent and 9 percent annually

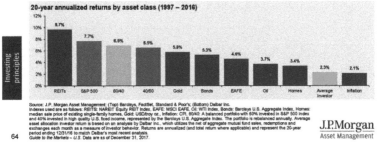

Source: J.P. Morgan Asset Management and Guide to the Markets [Q1 2018]

Chart that we use in presentations.

over that twenty-year period. I hope that you would be quite content with that type of return. I certainly would be!

For most investors, however, that's not what happened. Look at where the average investor is on the chart. (Spoiler: all the way on the right!) The average investor underperformed all of the asset classes they owned to a drastic degree...over two and a half times worse! So if the "average investor" had just bought all of those asset classes and then not made any changes, had they just stashed those account statements in a drawer and not looked at them (in jest... mostly), they would have averaged that 6 to 9 percent they'd signed up for. Instead, what did most people do? Maybe they chased the hot fund. Maybe they moved all the money in their well-purposed, diversified portfolio to the one stock that was doing well at the moment. Maybe, when the stock market lost 20 percent, they panicked, sold everything (thus solidifying the loss and making it real), and moved their entire account to cash. Then, they waited fourteen months to get back into the market, missing out on the entire market cycle recovery. Are you catching my drift here?

Let's take the last great market correction back in 2009 to bring home our point because it probably holds real meaning in your financial life. We all know how devastating 2007-2009 was for so many people. Maybe your parents and grandparents suffered as they entered their retirement years as a result of the recession, and maybe it was the first time you felt, firsthand, what it was like losing your hard-earned money in the stock market. You wouldn't be alone. Between March of 2007 and October of 2009, the stock market lost 57 percent of its value. To put that in context, if you had one million dollars invested in the S&P 500 in October of 2007, you would have lost over $500,000 in fifteen months!

Here's the reality though: if you had stayed the course, knowing that you didn't need the money anytime soon and that you could (and should!) wait out the market correction, you would be looking back a decade later in fantastic shape. Here's what Mr. Nick Murray had to say back in November 2017, "If you bought the S&P 500 Index in October 2007 (the peak of the market before the financial crisis) and held it until October 2017 (10 years), despite a drop of 57 percent in 2008-2009, your average annual return would have been +7.2 percent." (Nick Murray, November 2017.) But, as we already know, that's not what most people did! If you had gotten out of the market with the hopes of riding out the rest of the down market in cash before feeling more comfortable to reinvest your money, well, you effectively solidified that lost! Take a look:

The Importance of Staying Invested
Ending wealth values after a market decline

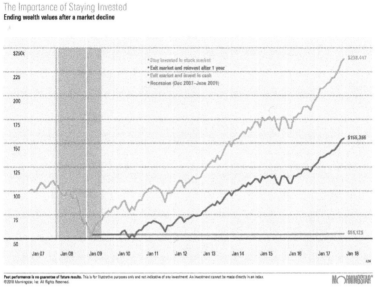

Source: J.P. Morgan Asset Management and Guide to the Markets [Q1 2018]

Think You Can Time the Market?

Let's take this a step further (just in case I haven't bludgeoned you enough with this idea). Some people come back to me (mostly my stubborn friends) and ask if all that emotional and behavioral stuff can be ignored if they know how to time the market, if they know when to get out right before the market downturn and then when to get back in before the stock market rallies. Resisting the urge to roll my eyes so far back into my head that I can actually see behind me, I immediately offer them a job on our team. Since nobody in history has been able to predict market timing with any measure of consistency, if *they* can, we want them on our team! Sarcastic or not, what I'm saying is true! If there was someone out there who knew, *truly* knew, what was going to happen and when, wouldn't we all just invest all of our money with that person and go watch Netflix?

Whenever this subject comes up, I punctuate my Netflix argument with the following chart.

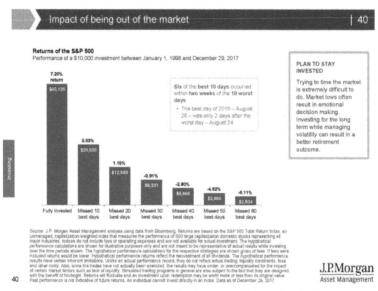

Source: © 2018 Morningstar, Inc. All Rights Reserved. Reproduced with permission.

So if you think you can time the market, I say you had better have a real quick trigger and be able to spot the changes right away! Because as the chart shows, missing out on even the best twenty out of a whopping five thousand days available during which you could have been invested in the market means losing out on basically the entire market's upside. Instead of making 7 percent annually, you're down to an almost flat 1 percent, and as I said, that's if you miss only twenty out of five thousand days!

OK, I've beaten you down. You now know that this "market timing" strategy has proven impossible, and you've figured out that I'm not about to give you my surefire secret to make a killing in the stock market next week. But you should be ecstatic about this, because in the last two chapters, not only have we shown that market timing is impossible, we've also shown that it's not even remotely necessary to achieve investment success! This is huge. Achieving long-term investment success has nothing to with outsmarting the stock market or speculating on the short term market outlook. Haven't we just all agreed that investing in the stock market as a whole (not even trying to find the "best" stock, sector, or fund) and then staying the hell away from your statements has historically resulted in a 7 to 9 percent annualized return? Well, sign me up!

> This "market timing" strategy has proven impossible. Achieving long-term investment success has nothing to with outsmarting the stock market or speculating.

How the Financial Media Gets in the Way

We've spent the better part of two chapters now discussing the permanent trajectory of the stock market despite temporary (and ultimately irrelevant) declines, and I still feel like I should be spending about ten more pages hammering the point home (don't worry; I won't), because it's so counter to everything we hear, every day, from the financial media. Every day on CNBC, there's a new crisis du jour, with some fancy guy in a suit talking about why the stock market is going to go down, or why this fund is going to outperform that one over the next six months, or why this sector is headed for a crash, baby! I don't know why Dickie Vitale just popped into my head, but I've always thought he would be perfect for a position in financial media!

In fact, the next time you're at the dentist's office, flip through the financial magazines. I'm sure you'll find an article about the top fifty ways to get rich, or the one hundred best stocks today, or a number of other dizzying topics that do nothing but help sell a lot of magazines. The top fifty ways to get rich? I'm always baffled by that headline. Don't we really need just *one*?

Have you ever seen Jim Cramer's show, *Mad Money*, on CNBC? He rants and raves about "the next crash that's coming!" and "the stock you have to buy!" and "the stock that's headed for a fall!" The show is brilliant in creating the sort of environment that keeps its viewers titillated. If you've seen the show, you've probably noticed that Jim never has any guests. This positions him as the ultimate authority, the one we have to accept and depend on. Look at the show's colorful set: all reds and oranges. It's meant to get you excited, to raise your blood pressure, and to put you on high alert. Jim's always yelling, gesturing vigorously, and moving around the set. He's creating an atmosphere of chaos, excitement, and urgency.

Now, all of this is fantastic television from an entertainment standpoint. But how often do we actually think his stock picks are right and wrong? Like most people, I'm sure he has his winning days and his off days. Nobody is right all the time (or even a majority of the time), because if they were, again, we would all just want to follow them and they wouldn't need to advertise their "hottest tips" quite so often. All that much of the financial media does is agitate and confuse people about their investment priorities and portfolios, and make them think about their investments as if they were horses they're betting on rather than part of a diversified, balanced, and carefully thought-out strategy that's built for the long run.

If I Were on CNBC

My point is that the TV talking heads, magazines, fund managers, guest economists on the CNBC panel, and the like, have no vested interest in sharing the sort of behavior-driven and common-sense financial planning tips that we've been discussing here. Imagine if I appeared on CNBC to discuss the market and what's going to happen over the next six months. I'd be sitting on a panel, the camera would turn to me, and Steve—the host—would ask me, "Gideon, what do you think the market will do over the next six months? Give us your expert opinion!"

I'd lean back, comfortable in my chair, and laugh.

"Steve, thanks for the question, but honestly, I have no idea. Absolutely *no* idea! The next six months could be up 600 points or down 600 points, God's truth. But I do know that that next 6,000 points will be up. The stock market has lost 10 percent every fifteen months on average throughout history, but over that same time period, a span of over sixty years, the stock market has gone up by 150 percent. So all you people watching, if you can stomach the short-term volatility and don't need the money next year, go relax. Watch TV and crack a beer. You'll be fine."

My guess is that I would never be allowed back on the show. What would we talk about next week? Everything I said is going to be as true the following week, and the month after that: not great for content! Simply put, the cyclical nature of investing and historic undeniability of its upward trend aren't exciting, and they don't sell magazines.

Do You Watch the Weather Channel All Day?

Think about how this same phenomenon tracks with watching the Weather Channel. When you check your phone and see that the whole weekend is going to be around seventy-five degrees and sunny, that's probably the last time you're going to check the weather for the rest of the weekend, right? You're saying, "I got it. It's sunny. And it will be sunny tomorrow. I'm all set, time to tan!" People really only watch the Weather Channel when there is a chance of a storm, or rain, or snow. We want to know when it's going to start, when it'll end, how many inches there will be. Bad news keeps us engaged! It's the same reality with the financial media.

One of my dad's favorite stories is about a commentator on a financial news channel, an "expert," who was asked about what would happen in the market over the following six months. He puffed out his chest, sat up straight, and boldly proclaimed, "There will be a 20 percent market downturn. Mark it down. Guaranteed."

Well, six months later, there was no market correction. In fact, the stock market had actually gone up a tiny bit over that half year. Well, the host of the show couldn't wait to have this guy back on his show. He was going to bury him! How could he be that confident and that wrong? (He had obviously never been on Twitter.) So this expert comes back on the channel six months later, almost to the day, and the host is positively giddy at the prospect of calling him out.

"So, what do you have to say for yourself? You were wrong!"

The expert, smiled, almost chuckled, and answered, "Oh no. I wasn't wrong. I just got the timing wrong."

So the next time you turn on CNBC and they're talking about the last six *hours* of the stock market losing money, think about it. Is that information really meant to help you? Is it really going to tell you *anything* that you don't already have covered in your investment plan? Or is it just a way to keep you engaged by keeping your emotions on high alert at all times? Turn on ESPN, watch *Shark Tank,* or re-watch *Game of Thrones.* I promise it will be a better use of your time.

So what's the moral of my story? As long as we've done our field intelligence, i.e., we know what our goals are, what our plan is, and we know how long we have to bring the plan to fruition, we shouldn't be mistaking an innocent sound in the middle of the night for an attack coming across the border! This illustrates my reason for having shared with you my guard-duty story (beyond just getting to share another badass army story). Just like standing guard in a location in which you can't see ahead of you, any investment not tied to a plan is bound to fail. Just as we need a strategy in developing our budget and our saving program, we also need an understanding of our time horizon and our future goals when it comes to our money *before* we start investing it. That way, we're avoiding mindless panic and poor decisions.

8

Saving with Purpose:
Our Three Bucket Approach

*"The trick is to stop thinking
of it as "your" money."*
–IRS Auditor

A question we get all the time, particularly from people who don't quite understand what we do as financial planners, is some version of, "What's your average rate of return?" Now, let's start with the fact that money management—the actual investment portfolios that we manage for our clients—is only a small part of the work we do together. You know this already, as we're over halfway into the book and we haven't discussed investment strategies with any specificity.

Investment Planning Is Not Financial Planning

A substantially greater amount of our time is spent discussing our clients' goals, cash flow, their budget, their mortgage, their student loans, their educational goals for their kids; ensuring adequate insurance protection; and generating income, to name some.

The fact that there are so many different areas that are encompassed by financial planning is why we lay out the different elements of our Financial Life Plan to prospective new clients before even thinking about making any recommendations about their investments. In fact, It happens all the time that a prospective client comes in to discuss their "investments," and then they realize by the end of that initial meeting that there are five more pressing issues pertaining to their personal financial planning that they now want to discuss. But even when we reach the point of the process in which we discuss investment management with our clients, questions about our average return is *still* not going to get them the answers they're looking for! Why? Because every single client has different goals, time horizons, risk tolerance, and priorities when it comes to their investing. Consequently, there really is no such thing as our clients' average rate of return. Actually, there probably *is* a number that we could come up with if we tried; it's just not going to help a client identify what his or her rate of return will be if we were to start working together!

We're All Planning for Different Goals

At DWM, we don't manage money in one particular way because every client that comes to us for help has a different time horizon for which he or she is investing and different goals for what that money is ultimately designed to do for you. This will invariably determine the investment strategy and the sort of account that make sense for that client, and the type of returns that they can realistically expect based on those goals. The performance return for two unrelated clients I meet with on any given day may be totally different because they will be based on an entirely different set of criteria.

I know how this may sound like a dodge to you, and so now you're just waiting for me to give you a really accurate rate of return on which you can hang your hat. Nope. When clients ask me what our average rate of return was last year, I respond enthusiastically, "I have absolutely no idea. For some clients, it was probably really good. For some, it was a lot lower." If the prospect doesn't walk out of the room in a huff, I explain exactly what I'm about to explain to you, namely, the importance of understanding our own investment goals, priorities, and personal temperaments.

It's incredibly important that a client understands why we are so steadfast in our commitment to this truth: we don't manage money, but, rather, we manage our client's behavior, their penchant for risk, and their expectations. If we can build our clients a successful road map through our FLIP, keep them on the right path over time by reviewing the plan, and keep them from making those rash behavioral mistakes along the way that can devastate a financial plan, then they should be just fine. The investments are just the means by which we will achieve all that. That's it.

The chart of financial priorities on the next page from Christine Benz, Director of Personal Finance at Morningstar Research, perfectly illustrates this reality.

The purpose of the money (what that money is ultimately meant to be spent on and when that's going to occur) should drive our investment choices and, over time, whether or not we make subsequent changes to the portfolio. The idea that our money, and therefore our investments, should have a purpose at all can be a strange concept if you've never thought about it before. You may say, well, the "purpose" of my investment, smart guy, is to grow and increase my net

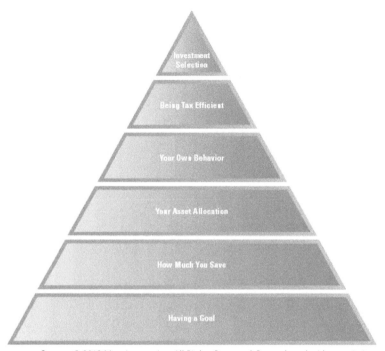

worth and make me rich! But as we discussed anecdotally earlier, that's not always the goal. This is why whenever we're creating a plan with a client, we divide the allocation of the amount they're able to save each month into three buckets. We call this (not so creatively I must admit), our Three Bucket Wealth Creation Approach. The buckets are the most clarifying way to illustrate the fact that we want different piles of money for different purposes depending on when we're going to ultimately spend that money in the future.

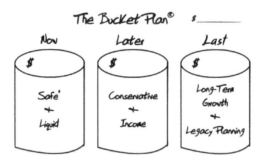

Trademarked original version of the buckets have been created by Clarity 2 Prosperity, LLC 2020; they refer to these buckets as "Now, Soon, and Later." We have used a three bucket approach since the beginning of DWM, but with the help of Clarity 2 Prosperity have been able to create a visual to our buckets.

As you can see, we've titled the buckets. "Now," "Later," and "Last" to make it clear as day that our time horizon with each pile of money will dictate the way the money is allocated between and within each bucket. Let's break each bucket down using some real examples from some clients of mine, so we're able to paint a realistic picture of what a comprehensive saving approach looks like.

One prospective client reached out to us, and said, "I have $100,000 sitting in the bank that I want to invest, but I'll probably take it out in the next six months to a year to buy an apartment. What do you recommend?" Well, we suggested that he shouldn't touch the money as we don't want to invest those dollars and, really, neither should he. Continuing on, we explained that he should be keeping his money safe and liquid in the bank until he puts a down payment on that home next year. Our reasoning was simple; those dollars needed to be available and accessible in the very near future and so it wasn't worth the risk to invest it right now. He was shocked that we didn't want to invest his money so we continued to elaborate. While the stock market historically trends upward, as we've discussed, there are short-term corrections all the time, and we can't predict if the market will fall again in the next six months. As we've explained, *nobody* can, and we don't want money that you need for a down payment in two months to be invested in a way that it can be decreased, even temporarily. That 20 percent decline is not temporary if you need the money now. Once you take that money out of the market (by selling out of your portfolio), well, now you have 20 percent less money available to you.

As such, this money needed to remain in his "Now" Bucket. Speaking more broadly, we recommend that all clients keep the equivalent of six months' worth of living expenses (could be more/less depending on your situation but this is a good rule of thumb) in the bank so that they could stay afloat for six months just with the money they have available on hand. So if you spend $5,000 each month, we'd want to make sure that you're building toward (or keep, if you already have enough cash on hand) about $30,000 in the bank. This money might become crucial if you were to change jobs and there are a few months before you find your next gig, or you decide to go back to school, or you take a sabbatical and travel to Thailand for three months, or whatever! Life happens. This bucket is called "Now," not because you're going to actually spend it *today* but because it's allocated in a way that will be available to you the second you need it at any point of your life.

Money needed for large expenditures in the next one to two years should also remain in our "Now" Bucket (we also call the "Now" Bucket your cash cushion). This money isn't instead of a six-month cushion, by the way, but in addition. If you're anticipating a large cost in the next twenty-four months (home purchase, engagement ring, grad school tuition, children's private school tuition, new business costs, etc.), you'd want to have money in the bank earmarked to pay for that specific large expenditure in addition to your six months living expenses that you are already saving (or have saved). The "Now" Bucket money is safe and accessible but comes with the tradeoff that we're not going to achieve much growth on this pile of money, but that's OK, that's what the later and last buckets are for.

Now, let's imagine that you're not thinking about buying that new home (or going back to school or starting a new business) for at least the next seven or eight years. Well then, your money can be invested more aggressively, as you have a longer time horizon before you will need to access the funds. As we've already discussed, the longer your time horizon, the greater likelihood that your investments will grow as you've given your money more time to rebound from any temporary market corrections. As such, this money earmarked for seven to eight years in the future, should be allocated to your "Later" Bucket and funded with investment vehicles designed to grow over time.

As you might imagine, money earmarked for your young (or future) child's college education (or camp, or parochial school, etc.) in ten to fifteen years would also fit our "Later" Bucket. Again, we wouldn't this money just sitting in our cash cushion as we know we are not planning to spend it any time soon and we want the opportunity for our money to work for us over the ensuing years. Of course, the investment allocation (percentage of stocks vs. bonds) within this bucket might be totally different depending on whether the money is meant for a home purchase in six years or your daughter's college tuition payment in fifteen, and for sure, the allocation would change as we got closer to each goal as well.

One of the most crucial pieces of the "Later" Bucket, and how it's most distinguished from the "Last" Bucket, is that the investment vehicles that we use for funds in the "Later" Bucket are needed to fund the financial goals that will come BEFORE retirement: flexibility is key. Our "Last" Bucket, on the other hand, is specifically and exclusively meant to be accessed *only* when we're much older. As you've probably guessed, this bucket largely consists of our various retirement accounts (401(k), 457 plans, SEP IRA, Traditional IRA, so on and so forth) and most of them have rules that make it counterproductive to utilize before we're at least fifty-nine and a half (penalties, taxes, etc.). Because we know for a fact that we can't touch the money in this bucket until that age, which for most of us is twenty plus years away, we can afford to be the most aggressive and growth focused with this money. Our time horizon has effectively wiped away any historical risk associated with investing in the stock market and so we want the reward (high returns) that comes with equity investing in this bucket.

Let's take a breath before moving on to discuss the actual sort of accumulation vehicles that would fit inside each of our buckets. First and foremost, I want to be really clear about one thing. The purpose of this chapter, and the surface level introduction to our bucketing approach and the sort of vehicles that fit inside each bucket, is not intended to provide you full clarity on what you need to do next. In fact, I've intentionally not spent a lot of time throughout the book defining the various types of accounts out there nor when or how much you should be utilizing them in your financial plan because a book, any book, should not replace the real comprehensive work that you need to do in order to build your financial roadmap. This should just be the start of a much deeper conversation on this topic.

That said, we do want to explore the ways in which we can be purposeful with the money that we're saving. Our desire to utilize tax-appropriate vehicles in our bucket plan is a great example of this purposeful and proactive approach. Organizing ourselves by the tax ramifications shown in the graph below is also a great way to introduce the various sort of vehicles that we could utilize as we build out our Financial Life Plan.

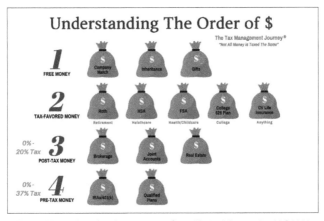

Created by and used with permission from Clarity 2 Prosperity, LLC 2020

Ok, so let's explain the graphic a bit. It goes without saying (though I guess I'm about to) that free money is the best money available to us and that we want to take full advantage of money that we're receiving with no tax "catch" coming due. This includes inheritances, gifts from family, and 401(k) matching contributions. When your employer matches a percentage of your 401(k) contribution, they're just adding money into your account: it's free money. It's for this reason that we recommend all of our clients contribute, at the minimum, at least as much money into their 401(k) as their employer is willing to match. If you don't, you're just leaving free money on the table that could be accumulating in your 401(k.) No one else is giving you that sort of deal!

Next, in the order of priority, is tax-advantaged money. In these types of accounts, your money grows tax deferred *and* you can take the money out of the accounts tax-free if you follow the rules. You don't get a tax deduction in the year that you contribute the money, but once the money is in your account, every dollar, including the growth, is yours. Roth IRA's, as we've already discussed, fit on this level as do Roth 401(k)'s and 403(b)'s, which work in the exact same way but are a part of your employment retirement plan. Most companies provide you with the option to contribute money into your 401(k) on a pre-tax basis (a traditional 401(k)), or a post-tax basis, (a Roth 401(k)) and you should absolutely be inquiring as to whether you have both options available in your plan.

Cash value insurance (as we're about to discuss in the next chapter) would be included on this tax-advantaged level, as are 529 Plans, Health Saving Accounts, and Flexible Saving accounts. One key detail to note that distinguishes Roth IRA's and cash value insurance from the rest is that these types of accumulation vehicles are more flexible: the money that you take out is tax-free regardless of what it's for. 529 Plans, on the other hand, offer you tax-free distributions only if the money is used for qualified education purposes, HSA's are tax-free when used for qualified medical costs, and FSA's are tax-free when used for either childcare or health care costs.

Most of these vehicles because of their tax efficiency and the fact that you can access them before you reach fifty-nine and a half means they could fit comfortably in our Later Bucket. The Roth IRA serves as the lone exception here. While it is true that you can take out your contributions (not the gains) to a Roth IRA at any point without penalty, the purpose of a Roth IRA is to help fund retirement goals. These vehicles are meant to fund our financial goals that may not be in the immediate future (under two years) but also aren't predicated on our retirement (twenty-five plus years). They're the goals that we're all thinking about as we go through our working lives (buying our first home, going to grad school, sending kids to school/college, buying real estate, buying a vacation home, starting a business, etc.) before we're in need of retirement income. Again, it's beyond the scope of our book how and when all of these vehicles fit together, but, simply from a tax standpoint, they are extremely advantageous vehicles that we want to at least be aware of.

The third level in the Order of Money is quite simple. This level chiefly entails brokerage accounts, investment vehicles that we'll refer to as post-tax investment accounts. If you have a brokerage account, you're only going to pay taxes on the gains in your account (because the money that you added has already been taxed before being contributed to the portfolio). So, if you were to put $250 into a brokerage account and it grows to $500, and then you decide to cash out, you would only have to pay taxes on the $250 gain. Even better, if you held the money for longer than twelve months, you wouldn't be paying taxes at your ordinary income tax bracket (which can be as high as 37 percent) but at your capital gains rate, which tops out at 20 percent for high earners.

Brokerage accounts also fit into our "Later" Bucket, as the money is accessible whenever we need it in the future and it can be invested as conservatively or aggressively as is appropriate for you. Most of the vehicles in the tax-advantaged bucket have a ceiling as to how much money you can contribute to them (which makes sense as they're vehicles that the government have given special and priority tax treatment toward... they don't let you park all of your money there!), but brokerage investment portfolios have no limits. As such, for high earners that are able to save a lot of money each year, brokerage accounts become an important accumulation vehicle in the later bucket as a way to invest and grow your net worth.

Lastly, in order of tax efficiency, is our pre-tax money that fits solidly into our "Last" Bucket...it's money that we can't touch until we're fifty-nine and a half without penalties and taxes (except for certain and very specific exceptions). It's helpful to think of pre-tax money as money that's held in partnership between you and the federal government. The government agrees not to make you pay taxes on the money as it's being contributed in return for their share of the entire account balance later on in life. I'll explain.

Pre-tax investment vehicles (a 401(k) or IRA) provide us with a tax deduction in the year at which we contribute the money to our account. For example, if you contribute $19,000 to your 401(k) in 2019 and your income is $150,000, then you would only be taxed on $131,000 of your total income this year: that $19,000 was put in your 401(k) BEFORE you paid taxes on it all. That's pretty cool. But it's the back end of the equation in which the federal government comes roaring back into your life demanding it's cut. Every single dollar that you take out of your 401(k) or IRA later in life is taxable at ordinary income rates. The implications of this fact can be devastating to our retirement.

When a retiree comes into our office and shares with us the exciting news that he has $2 million in his IRA, it's our job to make sure that he's aware of one unfortunate fact. Because that $2 million has never been taxed, if the client were to cash out his account (to buy a vacation home or whatever), he would have to pay taxes on the full $2 million at his ordinary income rate. This means that he essentially owes $600,000 to 800,000 to the federal government before he'll receive his own share, which will then shrink to about $1.2 million. So that gigantic $2 million 401(k) turns out to be little more than half that amount when it's all said and done. He never actually had $2 million, if we're being honest, because a big chunk of that money was essentially a liability that's owed to the federal government whenever our client chose to collect (his portion of) the money. Not only is the government getting its percentage of the money that you contributed along the way (which, to be fair, has never been taxed), it's also takes that same percentage of every dollar of growth along the way. It's for this reason that I like thinking about it as a partnership: this money is never entirely yours until you pay those taxes!

Not only that, but it's actually also a deal with the federal government that they can amend whenever they want! If tax rates increase in the future, well, then the federal government will own an even larger share of your pre-tax 401(k) or IRA. Most tax and financial professionals believe that taxes are only going to go up over time; our current tax rates are at their lowest ever and this low tax environment won't stand forever. Simply put, I don't want the retirement accounts that I share with the government to be dependent upon tax rates that are only going to increase with time.

There are ways to mitigate this problem even if the bulk of your assets are in pre-tax dollars. One such way is what's called a Roth conversion. This is a strategy in which you convert pre-tax dollars into Roth (after-tax) dollars by paying the taxes that you've been putting off as you contributed money to the pre-tax vehicle. This then allows you to benefit from Roth treatment in the account moving forward. I want to be clear that this is *not* always the right move. How such a strategy would impact your income tax bracket and whether you have enough cash liquidity to initiate this move may prove to make this strategy more trouble than it's worth for you right now. As always, my point is merely that we want to be aware of such opportunities and make our decisions as proactively as possible!

I'm going to be honest with you. I debated whether or not I wanted to include this entire conversation about tax strategizing and the specific vehicles we discussed in the book. It can get pretty granular and you're going to need to devise your own Three Bucket Plan and account for the tax ramifications there within, based on your own income, goals, opportunities, and personal circumstances

In the end, one thing brought me around to the decision to share it. So many people I meet are saving money into their checking/saving account, their "Now" Bucket—and to their 401(k), their "Last" Bucket)—but nowhere else. This isn't even unique to young professionals. Many American's have their wealth located in their pre-tax retirement dollars.

This means that millions of Americans are walking through life and into retirement with their largest investable asset co-owned by the federal government who is just waiting to take their (growing) portion...and most of those Americans don't even realize it! Ed Slott, called "America's IRA Expert" by the Wall Street Journal, and a nationally renowned tax planner, who specializes in tax strategizing and 401(k)/IRA planning, calls this the "The Retirement Savings Tax Bomb" for that very reason. His book *The Retirement Savings Tax Bomb*, dives into this entire area of planning in a lot greater detail and is mentioned in the Recommended Reading section in the back of this book.

All I'm saying here is that we do want to understand the tax efficiency of our assets and make sure that we're diversifying our tax strategy to utilize every sort of vehicle at our disposal. Hopefully this section makes you think about the ways that you're thinking about your tax investment planning (or lack thereof) and motivate you to do something about it. However, keep in mind that I've only gone into a high-level break down and should you want to explore the strategies and vehicles in more depth, and apply them to your personal situation, you should consult with a professional.

How Do You Feel About Your Investments?

As any good financial advisor will tell you having an understanding of your investment's purpose, time horizon, and tax consequences is only half of the conversation when it comes to determining an appropriate investment strategy.

The emotional makeup of our clients and the way that they think about money and their investments play a huge part in our approach to their investing strategy.

Two years ago, I met with a thirty-five-year-old advertising executive named Alison. She understood that she had a long-time investing horizon, she knew that being an owner rather than a renter (i.e.: owning stocks rather than bonds) would ultimately lead to higher investment return—all of the good stuff we've been talking about. Still, she told me, "If my account loses 20 percent, even if I know I don't need the money now, I'm going to be annoyed and won't be able to comfortably lay my head on the pillow at night!" Our knowing that about her changed everything. Again, we're not just managing her money; we're managing her behavior and her expectations. We were able to develop a more conservative portfolio than I typically would have recommended for someone in her age range because it fit better with how she thinks and reacts to her money. I knew that with the portfolio we created together, she would not panic and make emotional, rash decisions when the market went down, sacrificing everything she had built to that point. Instead, she was comfortable with her level of risk and would ultimately stick to her investment program, which is fundamentally more important than the actual holdings within her portfolio.

OK, so we acknowledge that your emotional tolerance as an investor, as well as your personal history as it relates to your financial world, are both immeasurably important in determining how you should be invested.

But how do we go about determining what essentially boils down to how you "feel" about money, risk, and performance? Here's what I think absolutely doesn't work: your typical risk questionnaire. If you've ever answered these questions for your 401(k), then you probably know what I'm talking about: questions that essentially ask you, "Are you feeling aggressive today?" and "Would you say that you're aggressive/medium/conservative in terms of risk?"

I'm only slightly exaggerating the ridiculousness of the questions on these risk questionnaires. The problem is that we all answer these questions depending on how we feel that day, which is almost always tied to what's been going on in the market recently (or heck, even if we had a good date the night before and are in a great mood!). If the market has been on a tear the last few months and you're checking your 401(k) each month as its value is increasing, you're going to answer the risk questionnaire by basically saying, "I *love* risk! Feed me more risk!" Alternatively, if your account has been losing money in a bad market, you're going to answer these questions by—understandably—claiming to hate risk. In other words, we all lie on occasion (admit it: most of you have bent the truth at some point in your life)!

What's Your Risk Number?

Our team has found software that we now utilize with all new clients that we believe gets past all of the BS described above to actually get to an honest conversation about your investing comfort level. I'll explain it here without getting too technical. The software asks you a series of fifteen questions, using the actual dollar amount that you personally have to invest to determine your "risk number." The fifteen questions are a series of either-or scenarios, like "Would you rather have a 50 percent chance of making 10 percent in the market, or a 50 percent chance that you either lose 20 percent or gain 30 percent?" The questions actually show you the real-world effects of those types of gains or losses before you choose an answer. Then, based on an algorithm of how you answer those fifteen questions, we'll arrive at your "risk number," which can be anywhere from 1 to 100. Just for context, a 1 means that you effectively should be hiding your money under your pillow (or in a checking account), and a 100 means you should invest all of your money in small-company stock out of a basement in El Salvador. The S&P 500, or the American stock market in aggregate, is about a seventy-three, just to provide some context.

Now, once you have your number, that doesn't mean anything right off the bat; you can't go walking up and down 5th Avenue waving around your risk number (I mean, you *could*, but you would just join the enormous list of crazy people shouting things on the streets of New York City). Your risk number becomes super important, however, after we stress-test how a portfolio with your risk number would have performed in the 2008 bear market or during the 2013 bull market (just two examples), and even more so when we compare your personal risk number to the risk number of your existing investments. Because if your risk number is a thirty-six (meaning you're pretty conservative as an investor) but your portfolio is a seventy-five, well, then, we have a problem! It means that your investments are way too aggressive for what you're comfortable with and that will increase your likelihood for panic, stress, and behavioral mistakes the next time the stock market falters! Again, we'd rather have someone's portfolio be more conservative if it means they're not going to behave their way out of long-term-investment success!

159

To be sure, this software we use is not the holy grail. It doesn't prepare us or our clients for everything; it's merely a starting point. That's it. The program does a great job of getting the client to think, *truly think*, about their investable dollars, what their comfort level would have been like while investing in different historical time periods, and what their goals ultimately are for this money now. I would say this is an even more important conversation to have with my younger clients for whom most of this talk about market returns, bull and bear markets, 2008, etc. is hypothetical. We weren't around for a lot of these historical time periods that we're referencing, and we didn't live through them, so it's tough for us to truly comprehend what it's like to be in the middle of such situations. Nothing compares to the real thing, but using real dollar amounts, money that you currently have in your possession, we will set the stage as best as we can!

Aligning Your Money with Your Values

Investing with purpose is a powerful thing. Sometimes, as we've established, it means investing in accordance with our time horizon and our emotional makeup. But it can also mean investing your money in a way that aligns with your values, passions, and convictions. This strategy is called Socially Responsible Investing (SRI), and it works just the way it sounds: you invest your money in companies that operate in ways and within industries that align with your own values.

Of course, we all have different values that we hold dear, and being socially responsible can mean different things to different people depending on our priorities. But not to worry—there are funds out there that focus on issues across the political spectrum, so it's just about choosing the approach that aligns with what's most important to you. Traditionally and typically though, just to provide some context, investing in a socially responsible way has meant investing in funds

> **Socially Responsible Investing (SRI)** means you are investing your money in companies that operate in ways and within industries that align with your own values.

that don't include companies that deal in oil, tobacco, and weapons and that have good track records on the environment and employee/worker conditions.

Investing With Our Values in Mind

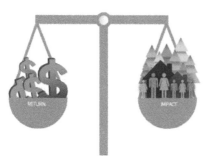

The simplest definition of "socially responsible investing" is that it aligns your money with your values and passions.

This approach has actually been around for a long time—about twenty years, in fact—but it's become a much more popular and common practice over the last few years as companies have become more transparent and we've all become more aware and confident as consumers with increased options.

Socially Responsible Investing has also become a much more appealing strategy, quite frankly, because doing so no longer means having to choose between being socially responsible or making money. Even a decade ago, to invest in a socially responsible way meant that you were probably leaving money on the table. Because there were so few options available and not such a strong demand, socially responsible funds were more expensive to own than other funds, and they didn't necessarily perform as well. As the demand has increased, however, the costs of owning socially responsible funds have come down, and it's no longer an and/or proposition. Or course, this correlation is kind of a chicken-or-the-egg causality dilemma.

As an advisor, if someone is interested in investing in a socially responsible way, I can feel confident that they can reach their financial goals in a way that makes them comfortable. I think that's a pretty cool thing. Of course, not everyone feels strongly about this, and as advisors, we're investment agnostic, but if a client wants to go down this road, we will help them get there. You, too, should know it as a viable option.

The Drucker Family Farm

When my dad steps away from Drucker Wealth someday, he wants to have a big farm somewhere out in the country. He wants to have cows, pigs, and chickens. (This is actually true, though I promise I'm arriving at a financial point here!) He wants to ride horses, hang out with his dogs, continue training in Brazilian jiu-jitsu, and spend time with his family. Even cooler (I think), he wants to build a compound that can serve as a safe refuge for veterans to recuperate, a safe environment for kids with special needs to have fun, and a committed training facility for groups of people looking to learn how to defend themselves, their families and their communities. This is his vision. He has always loved the outdoors and after a full career of working in Midtown Manhattan, he'll be ready whenever the time comes for this next great adventure. I have no doubt that he will create his perfect environment during this next stage of his life and that it will be as fulfilling and exciting as he imagines. But let's dig a bit deeper into this future Drucker Farm. Imagine that, on his farm, he can only have two animals: cows and pigs. Now, if he were to own pigs, how would he monetize them? What would he have to do? I'll accept as the correct answer your grimace and eye roll. Yes, unfortunately, he'd have to kill the pig, and he'd end up with bacon, ribs, and other cuts to sell. That's it. But then he doesn't have the pig anymore and so that would become the end of that story. Now, if he were to have cows on his farm, what could he do? That's right: he could sell milk! He could bring the milk to the market, buy more cows or more pigs, and keep the party going.

In terms of our investment world, when we talk about owning stocks, what are the pigs of our investment portfolio from the standpoint of how we can generate money in our pocket from owning them? Let me ask you this another way: If you own shares of Amazon, what do you need to do in order to make money? You can't bring your investment statement showing that you own shares of Amazon to the grocery store and use that statement to buy anything on your grocery list. It doesn't work like that—it's just a piece of paper. To be able to buy things using your shares of Amazon, you would need to sell the shares of stock and take the money—which is fine, of course, but then you wouldn't own the shares anymore!

Instead, what do some companies do that would allow you to actually buy stuff at the store without needing to sell your stock? That's right, they pay dividends. Dividend-paying stocks actually pay you to own them! For every share of a dividend paying stock like UBS that you own you would earn $4 in income without having to sell anything. Now, my point is not that dividend-paying stocks are better than growth stocks. In fact, for people our age, our fundamental goal is actually not to generate current income from our investments, but to maximize our growth and accumulation over the long term. So these growth "pig" stocks may actually make perfect sense for us right now, and dividend "cow" stocks may make sense later on in life. Regardless, my point is not that one or the other is *better*. My point, beyond just getting to talk about my dad's soon-to-be-epic farm, is to reiterate that our investments should have purpose at every step along our investment lifetime.

OK. We've discussed an investment's "purpose" from a few vantage points in this chapter: knowing the purpose for which you are ultimately going to use the money and having an understanding of your own risk profile and that of your portfolio, being chief among them. But this whole chapter, and really, our entire approach to our investment management, boils down to one question: Why do you own what you own? To me, having a solid answer to this question means having purpose to your investments.

9

You Don't Need a Protection Plan...Until You Do

"I made my money the old-fashioned way. I was very nice to a wealthy relative right before he died."
–Malcolm Forbes

Protection planning is the least fun part of wealth management. Nobody wants to talk about what will happen if they get injured, sick, or die. They certainly don't want to discuss the financial ramifications of any of those terrible things! Because of the understandable lack of comfort around this conversation, most young people don't even start learning about what forms of protection they need until it's too late (more on what this means in a moment). But any good financial plan must account not just for how to best climb up the mountain, but also what should happen if you run into problems and have to climb back down before reaching the top. In fact, this conversation should really be the first part of any financial plan worthy of its name because this foundation will prevent the collapse of every other part of the plan even if an emergency occurs!

What Does Insurance Do?

When I say protection planning, what am I talking about? Insurance! At its most basic level, insurance is a way of managing risk and protecting yourself from financial loss by paying for "someone" else (an insurance company) to take on the responsibility and costs of your loss. There is insurance for almost everything, even tickets to a nightclub (seriously!), but that's not what we're talking about here. In financial planning, we are looking to insure against losses that would devastate your family's financial plan. Chief among these are losing your life (life insurance), your ability to generate an income (disability insurance) and your need for hospital care in old age (long-term-care insurance).

The Younger, the Cheaper

Now, of course, not everyone needs all three of these types of insurance or even, necessarily, any of them! But I can say with 100 percent certainty that you should at least have an understanding of how these insurance products work and know whether or not you need them rather than dismissing/ignoring them out of instinct. The earlier you have this conversation and educate yourself on the different kinds of insurance policies out there, as well as their benefits and drawbacks, the better situated you'll be moving forward.

When I say protection planning, what am I talking about? Insurance! At its most basic level, insurance is a way of managing risk and protecting yourself from financial loss by paying for "someone" else (an insurance company) to take on the responsibility and costs of your loss.

For one, the younger and healthier you are when you buy life, disability, or long-term-care insurance, the cheaper it will be for you to get coverage. Insurance is based on actuarial science. If you are buying life insurance (which means somebody of your choosing will get a sum of money when you pass away), it will cost you less to purchase a policy when you're young and healthy because you're further away (statistically) from passing away. Most people are good with that explanation, but, if you're interested in knowing, the reason the insurance will cost less is because, from the insurer's point of view, they'll have more time with your money before they need to pay up. It's the same story when discussing your chances of getting sick or injured while working (which disability insurance protects against), or of getting sick later in life and needing hospital/home care (which long term care insurance protects against). Simply put, the longer you wait to buy insurance coverage all else being equal, the higher the cost will be for the exact same coverage. Each year that passes, no matter how healthy you might be, the cost to purchase whatever type of insurance plan you might want/need will rise.

When Is the Time for a Fire Drill?

More important than just making the cost of insurance cheaper, however, is this indisputable reason for having the conversation now: you don't want to have a fire drill in the middle of a fire. The time to think about protecting yourself and making sure that you're best prepared for whatever the future brings is before that random injury, sickness, or disability strips you of the ability to do anything about it. Over the past sixty years, we've had too many clients come to us later in life without enough insurance to adequately protect their family. Unfortunately, by the time they realize this, they're not able to get any more because of their age and/or health. That's why taking a comprehensive look at whether or not you need insurance is a crucial part of any financial plan right off the bat. None of my clients will ever feel like they didn't know enough or that their advisor wasn't open enough to have that difficult conversation about insurance before it's too late.

Without getting too deep into the insurance world, I'm going to describe the different types of insurance I mentioned in the beginning of this chapter so that you can start to get a baseline understanding of what they entail. This will be quick because, ultimately, you will have to get a more tailored analysis of how or why insurance may fit into your own family's planning, but we can at least set the stage with some high-level ideas and some real-life examples of protection planning.

Protecting Our Greatest Asset

For most of us young professionals, our ability to earn an income is our greatest asset: it's more important than any investment or savings that we own at the moment. This is only logical; if you're making $100,000 annually and you have another thirty-five years of working ahead of you; that's over $3.5 million in expected income, even if you were to never get another raise! That's a lot of money on the table, and we want to protect that golden goose (you).

For most of us young professionals, our ability to earn an income is our greatest asset. So think about what would happen if you were to get sick or injured—you would have no income.

Think about what would happen if you were to get sick or injured; you would have *no* income coming in each month and, I'd imagine, find yourself in dire straits sooner rather than later.

Having disability insurance means that if you are unable to practice your profession because of injury or sickness, the insurance company will pay you a designated monthly income (how much, when it starts, and how long the benefits will pay out for all depend on the details of the individual policy and are beyond the scope of this conversation). For this potential benefit, you will pay an annual premium to the insurance company for as long as you wish to maintain the policy. My dad has had his own disability policy since he was twenty-one, which means he has paid that annual premium every year for the past thirty-six years and has never once (fortunately) had to collect on it.

Some might say that it has been, therefore, an unnecessary expense—all those annual premiums down the drain! Well, first off, hindsight is always twenty-twenty, and if my dad could have foreseen that he wouldn't get sick/injured seriously enough to need it, sure, that'd be a fair point. But I appreciate the way my dad has characterized it: "Best thing

I've ever done. Every year I pay the premium, and I don't get sick. Happy to make that deal every time." Obviously, he's being facetious, and he's not staying healthy *because* he pays for disability insurance; that's ridiculous. His point is that he has never viewed paying for disability insurance as optional. If he were to get sick or injured and were without an income, it would be catastrophic. For him (and for me, at this point in my life), it's a no-brainer to protect against such a worst-case scenario.

1 IN 4 PEOPLE

WILL BECOME DISABLED DURING THEIR WORKING CAREER

Just over 1 in 4 of today's **20 year-olds** will become disabled before reaching age 67.

Source: © 2020 Texas Medical Association Insurance Trust

A lot of companies (particularly larger firms) offer disability insurance through work. Take it! If you pay for the coverage yourself through work, you'll receive the benefit (if, God forbid, one day you need it) tax-free. If your employer pays for your disability premiums, then you'll receive it as taxable income in that year. Regardless, it's a decision that's easy to make, as it's extremely inexpensive when offered on a group basis through your employer, and again, you're protecting yourself from the worst thing that could happen to you financially.

To dig a bit deeper, the reason that some clients of ours will purchase an individual policy outside of work is twofold. First off, once you leave that job and move to a different employer, you're no longer covered; the policy is not portable, and you're no longer protected. More important, however, is that most group disability plans limit your coverage up to a certain dollar amount. If you're a lower-paid employee, that's fine, as the limited amount would most likely cover your income as necessary. If you make a much higher salary, let's say $300,000, and are currently taking in $17,000 (after taxes) per month, and your company offered a monthly benefit up to $5,000 monthly, it would make sense for you to purchase additional protection to cover the gap because you would want to ensure that you wouldn't be in a $12,000 hole each month if you were to get sick.

Doctors and attorneys are particularly in need of personal disability insurance, as they are traditionally highly compensated and highly specialized, and so they are at greater risk of losing that high income if they were to get injured. They're also particularly vulnerable if they only have the group coverage that we just described. Most group insurance plans are defined as "any occupation," meaning the policy won't pay out if the client is able to do work of any kind, even if it's not the work that he or she is specifically trained for. This distinction is hugely important, as these group plans would *not pay out* if you were still able to work in a lower-paying profession (like being a greeter at Walmart) despite the fact that you can't do your actual job, the one for which you were trained.

Alternatively, individual policies can be set up with the definition "own occupation," which means you get paid the monthly benefit if you can't perform your specific specialty. To use a recent client example, a brain surgeon who is making $600,000 annually came to us because he wanted to ensure that he will be protected and provided for if he becomes unable to perform the daily tasks of a brain surgeon, because those specific skills are what afford him his high salary! If he were to injure his hands and could no longer perform surgery, but he could still teach, let's say, he wants to make sure that he's receiving payment for that huge gap between what he was being paid to be a surgeon ($600,000) and what he's now making as a teacher ($75,000), as a result of his injury. Therefore, he would make sure that he has that "partial disability" rider built in.

This is just one example. To be clear, we're just scratching the surface about the types, riders, and details of individual disability coverage. My intention here is simply to get you to the point of being able to think about what is, or isn't, applicable to your own life!

Protecting Your Family

For most of us, if we've given any thought at all to life insurance (and really why would we), we think about movies where the schleppy insurance salesman is pushing a policy on someone (Ground Hog Day in particular comes to my mind). The funny thing is…I bet that many (if not most) of the high income/high net worth people in your life own A LOT of Life insurance because they understand the power of tax efficiency and leverage when it comes to protecting their lives and their assets. Like with everything else, there are times when life insurance absolutely makes sense, and there are times and types that don't make any sense for your family's situation. Let's dig a bit deeper because I think a lot of the confusion over life insurance is about the two different types and what they do.

Renting versus Owning Insurance

There are two types of life insurance. The type you rent and the type you buy. The type you rent, called term insurance, is the most inexpensive way to protect your family for a given period of time (typically ten, fifteen, or twenty years). You pay a certain dollar premium each year over that designated time period—let's say twenty years—and if aliens were to come and take you away during those twenty years, then your family will receive a certain death benefit paid out to them. After that twenty-year period though, you no longer have that coverage. Essentially, you rented that death-benefit protection in the same way you might rent an apartment; once your lease is up, you no longer have that roof over your head. Term insurance is also similar to renting an apartment in that you're not actually building up an asset, as there's no money going back into your pocket after that twenty-year period ends; the money you paid was just an expense, like paying rent.

So why get term insurance? Term insurance makes sense if you have a young family, or have a large mortgage, loans, or other financial responsibilities over the short term, and you want to leave the most amount of money to your family for the lowest possible cost if you were to die sooner than expected. Term insurance then, is an emergency measure. It's taking precautions for *if* you die in the near or immediate future, and not *when* you die way down the road. Again, it's a great vehicle in the right circumstances, but it's not ultimately a true lifetime protection strategy, as a majority of people who have term insurance outlive those policies. In other words, there is only a small number of people who pay for term insurance policies and actually die during those periods in which they're covered, meaning only a small number of families actually receive money. I'm willing to venture that almost 100 percent of those people who had term insurance would do the same thing all over again to protect their family against catastrophe, but ultimately, it's not a realistic way to leave an estate or legacy to future generations.

Building a Non-correlated Asset

Permanent insurance, as opposed to the type of insurance that you rent, is more like buying a home. When you buy a home, in addition to having a roof over your head, you're also building up equity over time. Permanent insurance works in much the same way, as these vehicles have a savings component built in. In these types of policies, money accumulates in the policy like an investment account: down the road, you can take money out of the policy as you see fit. There are different types of permanent policies (Whole Life, Variable, Variable Life, and Universal) that affect how the money grows over time, but I don't want to make anyone's head explode, so I won't break each different type down.

Permanent insurance is generally more expensive than term insurance when it comes to getting the most death-benefit protection, just like buying a home is more expensive than if you were to rent a place. But in a similar vein, it doesn't really make sense to compare the two, because only by "owning" the coverage are you actually building up anything that you can one day sell, generate income from, exchange, etc. In other words, permanent insurance is not just a cost, but also a savings vehicle. In fact, for most of my H.E.N.R.Y. clients, we're not having a conversation about permanent insurance because of the death benefit (while important in the future, that's not so much the priority right now), but, rather, because of how it allows us to save and grow our own money over time!

I absolutely believe that permanent insurance has a place in a well-diversified savings program because it accomplishes a number of different objectives. It provides death-benefit protection at the lowest price you'll ever pay for it (because we're young), and it provides another way to automatically and consistently save money now, while giving you the option to extract your money from these policies in a tax-advantaged way down the road (remember, it's a part of that second level of tax efficiency in the chart from last chapter about the "Order of Money" along with Roth IRA's, Roth 401(k)s, 529 plans, etc.)

I own a Whole Life policy, a type of policy in which the cash value/savings portion grows in a way that's not tied to the stock market. I like the idea of having one conservative asset that isn't moving with the rest of my equity-oriented investments while accomplishing a number of other goals (death-benefit protection, long-term care access, automated savings, etc.). I especially like the fact that if I set up my policy the right way (according to the government), I will be able to take money out of my policy, later on in life, tax-free! For a lot of my higher earning clients that can't contribute to a Roth IRA directly anymore (because there are income limits) this becomes another tax-efficient vehicle we can utilize.

The cash value build up inside of a permanent insur-ance policy is also a powerful shield against the threat of sequence of return risk that can manifest at the point that we're ready to start withdrawing money from our investable assets. Understanding the ways in which sequence of return affects our planning will provide food for thought toward the way we think about our money for retirement in general.

At our age, while we're nowhere retirement and consequently not taking money out of our investments, the order of our annual rate of return doesn't actually matter.

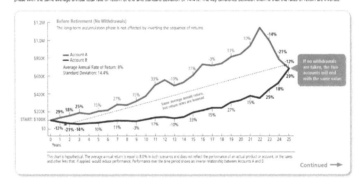

WHY THE SEQUENCE OF RETURNS IS SO IMPORTANT TO RETIREES

Most investors go through a life stage during which they make periodic contributions to their investment accounts, and then another stage—retirement—when they make periodic withdrawals. During retirement, the timing of investment returns can have a dramatic impact on a retiree's account.

Let's look at two hypothetical accounts representing the assets of two investors. Notice that although the accounts take different paths, they reach the end of the accumulation phase with the same average annual total rate of return of 8% and standard deviation of 14.4%. The key difference between them is that the rates of return are inverted.

Continued →

JACKSON®

Charts used with permission, © Jackson

As you can see, if you're averaging 8 percent annually, and not withdrawing money from your account, it's irrelevant whether you had great returns at the beginning of your investment period or at the end; you end up with the same rate of return and more crucially, the same dollar amount.

This chart illustrates why there is no sequence of return risk for us over the next ten to twenty years while we're in the accumulation stage of life. The sequence of our market performance doesn't matter.

The sequence of return risk becomes a real threat, however, when we get ready to start taking consistent withdrawals from our investable assets (like when we're retired and looking for our assets to replace our salaries.) When we're taking money out of our investments, it absolutely does matter whether the positive returns or happening at the beginning or the end. Take a look at the following chart.

The timing of distributions makes a difference.

Now let's look at two hypothetical accounts representing the investments of two retirees. Each retiree remains invested and needs to withdraw 5% at the end of every year. The starting point is the same for both accounts, but the end results are very different. The investor in Account A, who began the distribution phase in an up market, achieves an ending balance greater than when distributions began. But when rates of return are inverted, as in Account B, the investor taking the same 5% each year in a down market depletes the account by year 13.

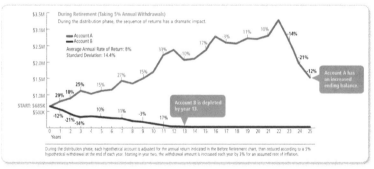

Are your investments prepared for your retirement? Work with your representative to find out.

JACKSON® | LONG-TERM SMART®

Charts used with permission, © Jackson

In this example, only one thing has changed: both individuals are averaging 8 percent and the order of the returns remain constant. But in this example, they're each taking out 5 percent from their portfolio every year. As a result, Mr. Unlucky ran out of money in year thirteen because he suffered negative returns early on!

Thinking about it logically, this actually makes sense. Mr. Unlucky is suffering losses when his money is at its largest value, so the losses are magnified. By the time he's back making gains, it's on a much smaller amount and so the gains are more peripheral. As he's also taking money out of his investments to live, it becomes impossible for those gains to get him back on track. Mr. Lucky, on the other hand, sees his highest gains on his biggest pile of money and so his later losses aren't enough to take him down.

This becomes a real risk in retirement, because we don't get to choose whether we're retiring into an up market or a down market. Some of you may have parents or grandparents that retired in 2000 or 2008 and understand exactly what I'm writing about. 2000-2002 and 2007-2009 both saw prolonged periods (thirty-eight months!) in which the stock market lost money. If you're in your early years of retirement when the stock market is down, we better hope that we have a strategy to ensure that sequence of return risk doesn't deplete our assets before we have a chance for the stock market to rebound.

As we've discussed in an earlier chapter, the stock market, based on all the available historical evidence we have, will rebound. The problem, however, is that if we're recently retired and drawing down on our investments, we may not have time to wait!

To bring this conversation back full circle, this is when having a non-correlated asset like cash value insurance becomes super important. If I'm unlucky enough to retire into a down period in the market, I like knowing that, I could take money out of the cash value in my insurance vehicle, in a tax advantaged way, mind you, while allowing my investment portfolios time and room to rebound before tapping into them. Simply put, the cash value in my insurance plan can serve as a hedge during a down market when I need to (or even just want to) take money out of my investments. It affords me flexibility to let my investments do what they were meant to do: grow unabated and unrestricted by my present day needs!

Reading that bit, you might be thinking, *well, that's a problem in retirement and you just told me that I don't need to worry about sequence of return risk yet, so why bother?* To that, I ask, how are you still reading this book?! Everything we're talking about is to set the stage for your financial success both now AND in the future; a little bit now goes a long way later. This is even more true in protection planning as all of the costs and benefits are dependent on your age and health.

We spoke a lot about having different purposes for our money. Providing flexibility and protection to balance my other investments is just one more example of this mindset.

Again, a further conversation is required to see if this truly makes sense for you. I'll just wrap up with this: Should you be putting all, or even most, of your money in permanent insurance? Of course not! But it does have a place, and again, I can only speak to what I do for myself: I bought my first permanent insurance policy as soon as I started making and saving money. And anecdotally, in our experience as a multigenerational firm, the people who most need insurance planning are the ones who blow it off initially, while the wealthier people we meet, typically, back up the truck to buy life insurance, understanding it as a financial instrument that can create and leverage vast amounts of wealth.

10

Do You Need a Financial Advisor?

"All coaching is, is taking a player
where he can't take himself."
−Bill McCartney, University of Colorado Football Coach

Here is what a competent, trustworthy, and committed financial advisor who cares about you and your family will bring to your world. He or she will sit down with you, with no predetermined ideas or judgments, and have an open, honest conversation about life. He or she will ask, gently, what keeps you up at night and what your greatest planning worries are. He or she will learn what makes you tick, how you grew up thinking about money, and what has changed over the years as you've begun working and started a family. He or she will ask about what excites you and what you're passionate about achieving in the next five years. He or she will ask you to share a bit about what a life without financial worries would look like for you and your family: Would you be doing something different? Would you volunteer more? What sort of legacy do you hope to leave when you're gone?

He or she will spend time creating a budget with you to strike the right (for you) balance between living the life you imagine and saving to defer some enjoyment for the future. He or she will create your savings program and then help you automate it so that you're putting money each month consistently and diligently, into the appropriate vehicles. He or she will show you what saving money will do for your future and continually motivate you to keep building upon what you've started.

He or she will review and revisit this plan with you early and often, so that two years down the road, when you may have switched careers, seen your income rise, or started looking for that first home, you will have planned and prepared effectively for that moment. He or she will help you adapt to your changing circumstances and show you what financial changes you need to make in order to stay on your goal-oriented road map. He or she will do his or her best to ensure, that if you get sick prematurely or pass away, your family will be taken care of, and while they'll be devastated, they won't have to think about the financial ramifications of the tragedy because he or she is there.

Over time, He or she will behaviorally coach you out of making the wrong moves at the wrong time for the wrong reasons in regard to your investments. This may be seven years out, when you're thinking about moving from your well-balanced, diversified portfolio in favor of the hot fund of the month that all of your friends are raving about. This may happen twenty-five years down the road, when the stock market is down 20 percent a mere five years before you're ready to take your well-earned and greatly anticipated retirement, and you call your advisor in a panic, proclaiming that you need to sell your investments. Your advisor will gently but firmly remind you that this, too, shall pass and nothing would be a surer way to devastate your family's retirement plan than to react to a temporary market swing. He or she will become a friend and a critic, an advocate and a coach, depending on what the moment calls for. He or she will attend your children's bar mitzvahs, confirmations, weddings, and graduations, as your family moves through life, and He or she will be there, always, to help keep you on the right path. Does that sound like someone you would like to have in your corner?

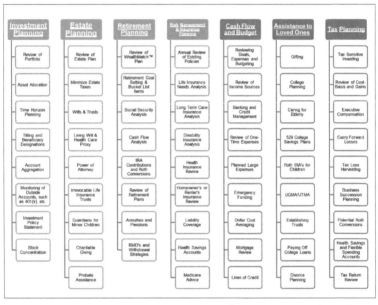

The most comprehensive visual I've seen illustrating everything that a trusted financial advisor will bring to your family's world.

Can You Do It All Yourself?

Here's the reality. Some of you will read all of that and think, *Well, I can do almost all of that by myself. Why would I pay an advisor to do it for me?* If that's your reaction, then truly, maybe you don't need an advisor. As my dad is fond of saying, if you have the time, energy, inclination, and knowledge to manage your family's planning, then you really don't need an advisor. Plenty of people do it themselves, and it seems to work out for them.

But I always come back to one point when I consider the merits of someone going at it alone: Think about the people in your world whom you consider successful, people who have accumulated substantial wealth. Do they handle everything themselves? Are they spending their days tinkering with their brokerage accounts, managing their retirement accounts, setting up their own 529 plans, and rebalancing their portfolios? I doubt it. In my own social circle, I can't think of too many people I look up to who don't have a financial planner guiding them and their family. Every successful person I've come across has become that way because they know what they're great at and what they can make money doing, and then they hire really smart people whom they trust to take care of everything else.

It's why my dad doesn't mow his own lawn, cut his own hair, or do his own taxes. He probably could do all of these things, but they would be a waste of his time and energy, and he wants to make sure they're done right. Isn't protecting and safeguarding your family's financial future at least as important to get right the first time as your haircut? (By the way, the joke about my dad cutting his own hair would work better if you could see the top of his head.) Simply put, a great financial advisor is your family's own insurance policy. You pay 1 percent a year to ensure that the other 99 percent of your net worth is taken care of for life.

How to Pick the Right Advisor

So what should you be looking for in an advisor? As you may imagine, I have some thoughts on what is most important in choosing a financial steward for your family's wealth.

Education

A starting point—a mere invite to the dance, so to speak—is evidence of a continued pursuit of knowledge in the various areas that are encompassed by financial planning like retirement planning, education planning, cash flow management, etc. It's important that the advisors you're looking at have specific certifications, such as the CFP®, ChFC®, CLU®, and RICP®, to name but a few.

Possessing these certifications alone certainly doesn't make an advisor the smartest person in the world, but it does show that he or she has gone a bit further down the educational path than others have. It shows a commitment to the craft as well as an understanding on their part that being an advisor is not just a passing phase, but, rather, their calling. If an advisor has gone the extra mile in getting these designations, it is far more likely that they will still be working with you and growing with you five and ten years down the road. They won't be working at an investment bank or have decided to become an accountant. I say that because these designations and the continuing education required to keep using the letters require a lot of time, money, and personal sacrifice. You should only be ready to commit to an advisor who is committing himself completely to what he or she does.

It extends beyond just the professional achievements of your advisor alone. I believe it's important that not only your particular advisor has relevant and impressive credentials, but that your advisor's entire team does as well, as it is likely that you will be working with them too. As our team has expanded over the last ten years, I've come to realize how crucial it is that every member of our team has a deep foundational understanding of what we do and how we do it. In fact, my dad encourages, funds, and motivates all members of our team to pursue any and every educational designation that will help them grow in their careers. Every single member of our full-time staff has at least one professional designation. This doesn't just apply to client-facing advisors, but also to our operations director, our client services managers, our financial planning managers, and our director of client event planning.

This focus on continuing education has obvious benefits to team morale and in creating a positive office culture, but I think it's an even bigger deal for our clients. When our director of operations is able to explain to them exactly how and when their money is being transferred, and can clarify the tax ramifications of their distribution without having to ask an advisor, our clients are comforted. When our financial planning manager can walk them through how to access and operate their client portal and link their outside accounts in one five-minute call, our clients are relieved. Having a team of experts benefits our clients in myriad ways, but for you, a young person seeking your own advisor, it's important to look for a team culture that values education and the pursuit of knowledge as a starting point.

Youth *and* Experience

One often-overlooked area of focus for a young professional looking for the right advisor is a balance between youth and experience in a firm's advisory team. You are not just looking for help over the next few years, but also over the next thirty, so it's important to know that your advisor is going to be there with you every step of the way while staying as committed as you are to the process. Here's a true story: a friend of mine who had been working with a family friend since before we met recently asked for us to take over his planning because the family friend had recently quit being an advisor in order to become a high school basketball coach! While I wish the new coach the best and personally hope he becomes the next Bob Knight, you probably want to find an advisor who is in it for the long haul!

As I've started working with a lot of my friends from high school and college over the last few years, I have realized how important it is for them to work with someone at roughly their same stage of life. Many of my friends used their parents' and grandparents' advisors throughout the first few years of their career, but they slowly started to realize that, ultimately, that may not be in their best interest. For one, a lot of them felt like they were being taken on as a client more as a gesture to their parents rather than because of what it meant for them as individuals. As a result, my friends weren't being made to feel as much a part of the financial planning process as they wanted to be. However much money they had that at that point was being managed, there was little personal planning for their individual goals, little explanation for what was to come down the road, and a deficit in the type of one-on-one attention that might address their personal concerns beyond their parents' and grandparents' objectives. To be clear, I'm not assigning any blame to their parents' advisors, who were most likely working for free and just trying to help the "kids" along as best they could. And at the end of the day, my friends were still being attended to, even on a basic level, in a way that most young people who are struggling along on their own are not.

That said, feeling like a third wheel in their own financial world began to weigh on them. Even more importantly, a lot of my friends realized that if their advisor was at the same age and stage of life as their parents, he probably wasn't going to be working in or as involved in the business when they are hitting their stride in their thirties and forties. The reality that they were at a different stage of life than the people currently helping them to plan for the future made them realize that they wanted their own trusted advisor who will be there when that future arrives.

One of my first clients and oldest friends put it even more succinctly when I asked him why he was so eager to begin our working relationship together: "My dad has had his advisor for thirty years. I've seen what their friendship and trust have meant to my own family over the years, and I want that same relationship with *my* advisor, someone who I like, respect, trust, and actually enjoy meeting with." Basically, beyond just the practical matter of differing ages, there has to be that personal connection and ability to relate to one other.

When I'm sitting across from my own H.E.N.R.Y. clients and showing them important ways to save for their first home, or discussing the importance of life insurance after they get married, etc., they know that these aren't abstract ideas to me. I am thinking about these very same issues and planning areas in my own life—which goes a long way!

You'll note that at the beginning of that youth-centric rant I mentioned, there needs to be a balance. While I believe having an advisor who you can relate to is important, I also know how crucial it is for that advisor to be a part of a team with older, more accomplished and credentialed advisors who have been down the path we're walking and know the way. On our team, for example, while I personally meet with all of my clients, all of the planning we do together goes through our director of wealth management, Kitty Ritchie, and our senior advisor and president, Lance Drucker. Collectively, they have over fifty years of experience in connecting and guiding clients. Having sat down with thousands of people over such a longtime frame, Kitty and Lance have a truly unique perspective when listening to a new client. They've seen firsthand all sorts of situations that can arise in a client's life. They've personally seen the ramifications for clients who get too emotional and move money out of their 401(k) and wait a decade to get back in. They've seen the consequences for young families that refused to acquire additional protection.

These stories and anecdotes become the armor and shield for clients today and tomorrow to avoid living through the same thing. We're able to anecdotally share stories and lessons when a client asks for our advice about refinancing their home, or needing a nursing home for their parents, or leaving a fair amount to each of their children, because, quite honestly, it's not the first time we're hearing those questions and living through those situations. It doesn't mean the advice is always going to be perfect, but it does allow for more context and clarity for the client to make the best decision for his or her family.

Simply put, experience matters.

I always think back to my first few meetings, when I was just starting out in the business. I frequently wondered to myself how other young advisors who were working for themselves had the confidence to even *want* the responsibility of handling a family's financial future. Right out of college, how could we possibly have the knowledge or experience to be the best advisor we will ultimately become? I spent two years learning every part of the business and sat in hundreds of my dad's meetings before ever sitting down with a prospective client on my own, so by the time I did create my own financial plans, I was more than ready. That's why I told all of my new clients in my first few years that not only was I lucky to be a part of a multigenerational wealth management firm with senior advisors manning the fort, but so were they! They would have the best of both worlds: access to the senior levels of one of the most successful wealth management firms in the country and the ability to work with an advisor who they like, trust, and could relate to now and in the future.

Being a Fiduciary

Sometimes buzzwords are just words that don't mean much. As Liz Lemon would say, "Synergistic collaboration is not a thing." But sometimes these words are talked about so much because they really *are* that important. Being a fiduciary is one of the important buzzwords! Being a fiduciary simply means that your advisor has to put the client's interests ahead of their own in all of their actions and recommendations. They can't do things for clients that are merely "suitable" or "acceptable," which is the standard that non-fiduciaries are held to; it must be in your "best interest." As I'm sure you can imagine, this is a big deal! To me, being a fiduciary is similar to the educational requirements that you should be looking for, in that it's a mere invite to the dance. Not everyone who is a fiduciary will be a great advisor, but all great advisors should be fiduciaries.

Along the same track of thinking, any advisor with whom you're speaking should have a clear and consistent breakdown of their fees. As with most things, the more complicated an advisor's fee structure and the more convoluted it is to explain, the less transparent the client-advisor relationship will likely be over time. I can only speak to my experience as an advisor, but when a soon-to-be client asks us how we get paid, they receive a clear and direct answer. We're not trying to obfuscate our fees or sugarcoat them. In fact, we're proud to explain our fee structure because we're confident in the value that all of our clients are going to receive when they commit to our process.

Likeability and Trustworthiness

The last segment of this episode of *The Bachelor: Financial Advisor Edition* is something that's difficult to explain, but I believe it is *the* single most important factor in determining whom one should hire as a financial advisor. Quite simply, you have to *like* and *trust* your advisor. You have to know that they genuinely have your best interests at heart and that they really are committed to and aligned with helping your family achieve its goals. Liking someone and trusting them are two totally different ideas, and they're each important.

Before you can trust someone, you have to like them. You don't need to be best friends (though I think the relationship will be much stronger if you are close), but there needs to be some connection there, some personal bond that draws you together (OK, now I really am turning this into an episode of *The Bachelor*.) This advisor is going to be an important part of your life. They will know some of your innermost goals, passions, dreams, and fears—and furthermore, they will be one of the most instrumental people in guiding you to and through fulfilling them. There should be a warm, positive feeling when you meet, and while this probably won't happen in a first meeting, getting an idea if this is someone you like and feel good around is important for the long-term health of the relationship.

This connection goes both ways. One of the things I'm most proud of in my career thus far is how many of my high school friends and college buddies have turned to me in the last few years to assist them with their planning and help manage their investments. It means a lot that these people who know me best are so confident in my abilities and eager for me to safeguard their family's financial life. It is truly the greatest compliment in the world.

Take that First Step into Your Future

When I sit down with a new and prospective H.E.N.R.Y. in my office or on our first Zoom call, I am aware that this might be the first time in their life that they've met with a "financial advisor" and, for many, the first time they've really looked at their financial future as something worth "planning for." As with any unknown, but especially for something as daunting as money, investments, and "the stock market," this can make for an intimidating and anxiety-inducing atmosphere the first time around. I see my role with so many of these prospective H.E.N.R.Y. clients as getting them to the point of being comfortable "enough" in the following areas: the concept of planning in and of itself, articulating their goals and their costs; and with investments, budgets, and insurance. I want "finance" to lose its intimidating mystique, because only then can they contemplate action.

More than anything else, I want those H.E.N.R.Y.s to feel empowered.

Empowered to make active and conscious decisions in their financial life.

Empowered to chase after their financial goals and dreams. Empowered to know that their future selves will thank them for taking that first step today.

But, paradoxically, to get them there, to get them to "act," I also need to create a sense of anxiety. Some level of anxiety and stress is not a bad thing. It's what forces us, all of us, to take action. It may be as simple as realizing, *Woah, I really do need to start thinking about when I can buy my first home* or *Wow, I need to check what my 401(k) is invested in* or *I need to have a better idea of how much I'm saving each month.* The impetus can be anything, but in our experience, there has to be something that forces us to take control of our financial life; we, as a people, don't challenge ourselves or make changes when we're content with just gliding by. We need a catalyst.

That's what (I hope) this book becomes: a catalyst. If I've done my job correctly, you should have a lot more questions about all of these topics than you did when you started reading! Your head should be moving a million miles a minute. You should be motivated to gain more knowledge. To talk about money more openly. To speak with your parents about their successes and failures over the years. To write down your goals. To get excited about what your future holds in store. Because this is just the start.

Final Thoughts:
The Dad Gets His Final Say

It's with great pleasure (I am his dad, for God's sake) to find myself writing the epilogue for a book written by the third generation of the Drucker family: Gideon. To say that I am overwhelmed by what this kid has accomplished in his twenty-eight years on this earth is a bit of an understatement—scholar, athlete, paratrooper, and now author and director of the Wealth Builder division of Drucker Wealth. I have watched history repeat itself, as I, too, once sat at my dad's table listening to his stories of clients who did the right thing (and of those who didn't). When Gideon was young, I shared with him my clients' stories of success as well as the (mostly) behavioral mistakes they made along their financial journeys.

Gideon completed his CFP® certification in approximately eleven months. Per the College for Financial Planning, the average time to achieve this certification is *three to four years*. When I asked Gideon what his rush was, he replied, "If my clients are going to depend on my advice and knowledge, then I'd better make sure I know of what I speak."

Yeah, I sleep pretty well at night knowing that someone who shares my last name is prepared to take over the reins in the not-so-distant future. If something were to happen to me, he is the man I'd want to handle my family's finances. I have no greater compliment. I hope you have enjoyed his words of wisdom...most of which he stole from me!

— Lance Drucker
President of Drucker Wealth Management,
Second-Generation Drucker, Proud Dad

Recommended Reading

1. *Simple Wealth, Inevitable Wealth* by Nick Murray
2. *The Millionaire Next Door: The Surprising Secrets of America's Wealthy* by Thomas J. Stanley and William D. Danko
3. *The War of Art: Break Through the Blocks and Win Your Inner Creative Battles* by Steven Pressfield
4. *How to Avoid Bag Lady Syndrome (B.L.S.): A Strong Woman's Guide to Financial Peace of Mind* by Lance Drucker
5. *Think and Grow Rich* by Napoleon Hill
6. *Grit: The Power of Passion and Perseverance* by Angela Duckworth
7. *Make Your Bed: Little Things That Can Change Your Life...And Maybe the World* by Admiral McRaven
8. *The Retirement Savings Time Bomb...and How to Defuse It: A Five-Step Action Plan for Protecting Your IRAs, 401(k)s, and Other Retirement Plans from Near Annihilation by the Taxman* by Ed Slott

9. *Stocks for the Long Run: The Definitive Guide to Financial Market Returns & Long-Term Investment Strategies* by Jeremy Siegel

10. *The Bucket Plan: Protecting and Growing Your Assets for a Worry-Free Retirement* by Jason Smith

11. *Exodus: A Novel of Israel* by Leon Uris (the book that inspired my other lifelong passion and pursuit)

12. *Harry Potter* by J.K. Rowling (Indulge me!!)

Acknowledgments

I want to give a hearty thanks to Sara Stratton and her whole publishing team…all of whom have been absolutely amazing from day 1 of this project…Writing a book, especially for the first time, can be (and was) an intimidating & relentless endeavor…but you've made this process as smooth and easy as possible…Sara, thank you for all of your hard work, notes of confidence, and for being someone I could trust and count on throughout….I truly appreciate it all.

I want to thank the entire Drucker Wealth Team…Neisy, Priya, Bridget, Giselle, Kitty, Lance, Beth & Mickey…I realize how fortunate I am to get to come to work every day with people that I consider friends & family. I truly appreciate all that you do…& I get excited just thinking about what the future has in store for all of us as we grow together.

A special shoutout of thanks to Bridget Farrington, our Director of Wow, who has been my go-to friend, resource, confidant, and motivator over the course of this whole book writing journey...I think I could have written this book without your help; it just wouldn't have been done for another thirty years. Bridget, thank you for making this book a reality.

Thank you to my sister Gabby.... who is my confidant in all things and who might have read the manuscript about twenty-three different times throughout the past year...I know I can count on you for anything & I love you bachi.

And to my mom (Ima) and dad (the big guy), a mere "thank you" for help with my book seems a bit ridiculous to be honest....but like with anything else in my life that I'm proud of or thankful for, I couldn't have gotten this done without your love, support, and unwavering belief... thank you.

Endnotes

Chapter 1:

1. Hoffower, Hillary. "Meet the Average American Millennial, Who Has an $8,000 Net Worth, Is Delaying Life Milestones Because of Student-Loan Debt, and Still Relies on Parents for Money." Business Insider. Business Insider, December 25, 2019. https://www.businessinsider.com/average-american-millennial-net-worth-student-loan-debt-savings-habits-2019-6.
(Please note that all statistics shared on bullet points on pages 9 – 10 share the above citation)

Chapter 2:

2. Information in chart sourced from Glassdoor.com, credit: Jack Kelly. Chart designed by it_solution_hub for this book. https://www.glassdoor.com/List/Highest-Paying-Jobs-LST_KQ0,19.htm.

Chapter 4:

3. Information for first chart on page 73 sourced from collegeboard.org. Information for second chart on page 73 sourced from Federal Reserve Bank of New York. Chart designed by it_solution_hub for this book.

Chapter 5:

4. Information for chart on page 87 sourced from HowMuch.net, a financial literacy website, credit: Raul. Chart designed by it_solution_hub for this book. https://howmuch.net/articles/buy-home-50-largest-metro-areas.

Chapter 6:

5. Nick Murray, July 2017- data sourced from S&P, National Bureau of Economic Research, US Bureau of Economic Research.

6. Nick Murray, July 2017- data sourced from S&P, National Bureau of Economic Research, US Bureau of Economic Research.

* Morningstar charts (pages 110, 113, 119, 132 and 143) disclaimer. © 2020 Morningstar, Inc. All Rights Reserved. The information contained herein: (1) is proprietary to Morningstar and/or its content providers: (2) may not be copied or distributed; (3) does not constitute investment advice offered by Morningstar; and (4) is not warranted to be accurate, complete or timely. Neither Morningstar nor its content providers are responsible for any damages or losses arising from any use of this informa-tion. Past performance is no guarantee of future results. Use of informa-tion from Morningstar does not necessarily constitute agreement by Morningstar, Inc. of any investment philosophy or strategy presented in this publication.